My Story And The Three Christians Who Transformed My Life

THE TOUCH OF CHRIST

ABDUL SHAKUR

The Touch of Christ

My Story And The Three Christians Who Transformed My Life

ABDULSHAKUR ISA

ISBN: 9798847725859

DISCLAIMER

This publication only offers general guidance, not specific advice. Your goals were not taken into account when it was being prepared. Before taking this suggestion, you should think about whether it is acceptable in light of your own goals.

Additionally, not all of the lessons I've shared in this book may concur, conform, or be in line with the expert teachings; but, since everything I say is based on my personal experience, it neither makes it right nor wrong; it just makes it my experience. And all I'm able to do is speak from my own experience. As a result, I rely on you to include what is helpful, discard what isn't, and add what is uniquely your own.

So, if you wish to apply the ideas contained in this book, you are taking full responsibility for your choices, actions, and results. Therefore, if legal advice or other expert assistance is required, the services of a competent person should be sought.

Good luck

WHY DID I WRITE THIS BOOK?

I've heard countless tales of people who started out with a promising future but ended up in a slump. I hope that my story will inspire someone to make a shift in their mental structure and get them back on track to a brighter future.

Over the last decade, my mission has been to be a source of motivation and encouragement. To help people find their purpose and tap into their passion, to help them hone their vision and strive toward their goals. I believe there is no greater joy and fulfillment in life than seeing others blossom, grow, and reach their potential through you.

In my past life experiences, I've picked up key lessons and principles that have helped turn me from a wayward youngster to a more disciplined, more focused, and more responsible adult, which I've shared in this little book. In this book, I'll be sharing with you a new perspective and a system that shows you how to think differently.

I hope that this book will not only give you a new perspective or at least a mild shift in your thought structure but, more importantly, a road map to implement everything you've learned from your own unique experiences in the past and connect those learnings in a clear, concise manner for a better future.

I came into this world crying while others were smiling... I hope that, at the end of my life, I shall leave this world smiling while others cry.

DEDICATION

To my father, Alhaji Isa Jibrin, a man with a large heart who stood by and helped me through the difficult times, you are my hero.

To my dear mother, Hajiya Zainab Isa, without whom I would not have understood the wonder of love.

To my stepmother, Hajiya Maryam Isa, thank you for your encouragement and financial support. You are a mother every other mother should emulate. You deserve the best life has to offer.

I hope that Allah's favour and mercy be upon my grandma Khadijah Ibrahim, who I wish was alive at the time I was penning these lines.

To all the great men who persevered through

difficult circumstances, I know you are better because you didn't give up. I am aware of the burden you bear, and I honor you for making the sacrifices necessary to become the man you are. This is my homage to you.

ACKNOWLEDGMENT

The most difficult part of this book is the acknowledgments. There are so many people who played a vital role in making this book a reality that I would love to acknowledge. I have been blessed with so many wonderful people who have made a huge and massive impact on my life—that trying to name them all can take an entire chapter.

I feel incredibly lucky to have so many wonderful friends, but I'm afraid I'd leave some out if I tried to list them all. Instead, I will simply express my gratitude to God for those unique individuals who have greatly improved my life. I appreciate all of your thoughtfulness, well wishes, and prayers over the years.

I am extremely grateful to you because you were the impetus I needed to make a significant change in my life. Without you, I would be severely undernourished on the inside and grossly underdeveloped on the outside.

However, the following individuals fall into a distinguished category that deserves mention: Alh.

Usman Ukandu, Alh. Abdulkareem Nuhu, and Engr. Muhammad Kabeer (you have been my mentors and a father figure that I learned from as I grew up). I am thankful for the friendship we have—a friendship filled with deep and transparent conversation. It has been therapy for my soul. Perhaps, you cannot even explain in what way you've influenced me.

I would like to deeply appreciate the efforts of a woman who has been my backbone in times of need, a woman who stood with and by me through thick and thin, in times of deep and pressing financial need—Mommy Favor, words cannot express the gratitude and esteem I have towards you.

Khalid Abdul Wahab , my dear friend and brother, your unwavering support and encouragement to me over the few years we've known each other are immeasurable. You hold a special place in my heart. Paul Obadiah, I honor and respect you a lot. You've been a source of inspiration to me. You were a light in the dark, a lamp on my path. God bless you greatly, brother.

To my brother, Usman Dundere, words alone cannot express the gratitude I have towards you; you are a brother that I revere and respect a lot.

Your light will never go dim. Thank you for your support and love. I deeply appreciate you.

Musa Adamu Ndawayyo, I deeply appreciate your support and the impact it has had on my life. Without your input into this project, this book will have not seeing the light of the day. A thousand pages are not enough to express my gratitude. Thank you.

Thank you so much! To Billal Wakil and Baisa Mallah, I say God bless you greatly for your support over the years. To my friend and brother, Hafiz Adamu, thank you for your love, kindness, and support in my life. You have been a pillar to lean on in tiring times. And to many others that I may not be able to mention, I say thank you all so much.

Fatima Garba, a truck load of gold and silver cannot express how much I appreciate your contribution to my growth. Thank you.

To my siblings, Zainab, Khadijah, Halima, Hauwa'u, Rukayya, khadijat and Ummu Salma. If I were given another chance to choose siblings, I would have chosen you ten thousand times.

Contents

DISCLAIMER iv

WHY DID I WRITE THIS BOOK? v

DEDICATION vii

ACKNOWLEDGMENT ix

INTRODUCTION xvi

ISLAM BY BIRTH xix

SEVEN YEARS OF BATTLING ADDICTION xxvii

WEIRD CHILDHOOD xli

STAY YOUNG AND USEFUL liii

ATTITUDE MAKES THE DIFFERENCE lv

GOOD WISDOM COMES FROM GOOD LISTENING, NOT GOOD TALKING lxii

THE COMMAND SAYS "Give!" NOT JUDGE lxiv

IT COST YOU NOTHING TO BE KIND lxxv

PRESSURE CREATES A DIAMOND lxxvii

MY FIRST JOB INTERVIEW lxxxix

A GIFT OF FAILURE xcix

LET LIFE STING YOU FOR A LITTLE WHILE ciii

NEVER SHY AWAY FROM YOUR IDEAS cv

GOLDEN "A" cviii

LIGHT YOUR CANDLE cxxiii

DEFY THE STATUS QUO cxxvi

LOSERS CAN'T DEFINE WHO YOU ARE cxxxiii

RESENTMENT IS THE ATTRIBUTE OF THE WEAK cxxxv

THE TOUCH OF CHRIST cxl

IT'S NOT TIT FOR TAT cxlii

DREAM SABOTEURS cxlvi

CAPITALISE ON YOUR MISTAKES cli

PRIORITY clxii

BE ACCOUNTABLE BE RESPONSIBLE clxviii

GO FOR CHARACTER OVER REPUTATION clxxi

A BILLION-DOLLAR QUESTION clxxxi

RECOMMENDATION clxxxv

INTRODUCTION

I am not sure how you stumbled on this book. Perhaps you purchased it or someone gifted it to you. However, the fact that you're reading these lines proves that dreams do come true and that nothing can put a stop to an idea whose time has come.

My burning desire has always been to do something that can change lives for the better, to be a source of inspiration, motivation, and hope to many people. This passion has led me to attempt many things over the years—some of which have succeeded and some of which have failed.

A few years ago, some people who had heard me tell my story at various events approached me and encouraged me to start writing. I was, however, hesitant for some reasons. Firstly, I thought the timing was not right—and secondly, I had earlier had a bitter experience that made me think writing is not for people like me.

These two occasions made me freak out when I thought of writing my book. However, deep down, it was what I wanted and desired passionately. On multiple instances, if we got into a long conversation with someone and I ended up telling them about my life's path, the conversation usually ended with a sigh and the comment, "What an incredible story! This is a lesson that can be drawn from, as you have much to say about life."

I frequently use my personal experiences to discourage people from doing something that I believe will ruin their lives. I occasionally receive a positive response, occasionally a negative response, and occasionally received the awkward remark, "Well said motivational speaker."

However, the majority of the time, the folks who make fun of me come back to say, "You know what? You were right. I was never wise enough to anticipate how things would end up. Thank you!

Relative to where I started in life, I never thought in my wildest dreams that I would be doing some of the things I'm doing today. But I'm committed to giving my best possible to the service of mankind such that when I'm gone there will be a vacuum.

ISLAM BY BIRTH

My name is Isa AbdulShakur. I'm a Muslim from the Northern part of Nigeria. I have been a practicing Muslim my entire life. My entire life has been spent in the North. I have had a genuine and sincere connection with members of other faiths. Most of the time, though, I hear people arguing over religion or faith, with each side arguing that their belief system is the only one that truly leads to God.

These disagreements can occasionally result in violent conflict and tragedy. I used to fall into the category of "religious extremist." But as I grew older, I began to see life and religion from new perspectives, and I gained a new understanding of both. It takes more than displaying charisma, strength, or energy to be a pious Muslim or a devoted Christian.

I have been wronged, cheated on, and lied to by individuals I believe to be pious Muslims and I have been wronged, cheated on, and lied to by individuals I believe to be devoted Christians. Neither Muhammad nor Jesus promoted or encouraged any of these negative traits when they were alive. Instead, they violently kicked against these ungodly traits.

The reason for this is that after studying the lives of Jesus (AS) and Muhammad (SAW), I discovered some traits in their leadership and behavior that helped both honorable and respectable men gain the following they do today.

For that reason, I'm calling on everyone out there to be a good Christian or Muslim if they identify as such. Be a decent Christian if you identify as one. Be a decent Muslim if you practice it. After that, I also want to add, regardless of which religion you're practicing, be a good advocate for it.

Because 99 percent of Christians don't read the Qur'an, in other words, the Qur'an that Christians hear about is you, the Muslim. Similarly, 99 percent of Muslims have never read the Bible, and what they know about it comes from you, the Christian. Others evaluate your faith based on your personality and character. Don’t give others a bad image of your belief.

While there is no disputing that Islam and Christianity are the two most prevalent religions practiced in Nigeria and throughout Africa, I'd also like to introduce to you the third major religion, known as the "Confusionist" religion.

These groups of individuals are neither Christians nor Muslims. They tend to be more prevalent among those whose parents practice a different religion. If one parent moves away or gets divorced, and one parent resides, let's say, in the North and the other in the South, he is Moses in the South and Musa in the north.

They spend the first 20 years of their life primarily in a state of confusion, and when they finally reach adulthood and decide to commit to one faith, they are likely to choose the parent with the better financial standing.

In essence, people don't make decisions based on conviction. Rather, they make decisions based on circumstances or origins.

You might find this heartbreaking because their situation is so obvious, but the majority of us are just like these people. The majority of us found ourselves in the religion we practice today. In other words, we're either Christians or Muslims by default (not our choice). But, why am I saying all this? Hang on. I'm taking you somewhere.

If you're a truth-seeking interested person, as I have been, then I urge you to set aside a few minutes every day of your life to consult holy books as well as listen to preachers and clergymen from both religions that preach the word of God.

I've come across upright, honorable, and devoted Christians who have earned my deep admiration for their teachings, values, morals, and ethics. Clergymen like Dr. Myles Munroe, Bishop T.D. Jakes, Nick Vujicic, David Oyedepo, and Apostle Joshua Selman, among others.

So also, I've met Muslims whose personality traits, morals, character, ethics, principles, and teachings moved me to tears. Preachers like Dr. Zakir Naikh, Ahmad Deedat, Mufti Menk, Al-Garqawiy, Imam Umar Usman Baba and so forth...

However, the ones that strike me the most are those individuals who were raised in one religion but later converted (on their conviction) to another faith (from Islam to Christianity or vice versa) and clung to it tenaciously.

Some examples are Khalid Yasin (USA), Cat Steven (British), Yusuf Estes (USA), and Aminah Assilmi (USA).

I've been exposed to so many things in my quest to seek the truth that sometimes I look up to pray to the Lord, "Lord, I hope I'm on the right path," every now and then I ask myself. "What if I die today and wake up believing in something other than God?" God then questioned me, "Did you not get my message?" And what did you say and do about it?

This is because… I don't believe God put us on the planet earth to live, eat, sleep, have children, and die, and then rewards us with paradise for doing nothing.

I don't think God sent prophets to simply teach us Hebrew, Arabic, and other languages to demonstrate our intellectual prowess or linguistic diversity. I don't believe God relocated Adam to earth for the purpose of exposure.

For this reason, I formulated some phrases I use to communicate with my creator, with the hope that he guides me down the right path. I hope you will follow suit.

Prayer sample

- GLORY BE TO YOU, LORD OF ALL HEAVEN AND EARTH.

(Notice: I didn't say Allah, Jehovah, Elohim, Shaddai, or God. It's intentional.)

- ALL PRAISE IS TO THE CREATOR OF MANKIND AND ALL THAT EXISTS.

- THE MOST GENEROUS AND MOST MERCIFUL.

- YOU ARE THE ONLY OWNER OF THE DAY OF RECOMPENSE.

- THERE IS NO OTHER WORTHY OF WORSHIP ASIDE FROM YOU.

- GUIDE ME TO THE STRAIGHT PATH.

- THE PATH OF THOSE UPON WHOM YOU HAVE BESTOWED YOUR GRACE, NOT IN THE MANNER OF THOSE WHO EARNED YOUR ANGER, NOR IN THE MANNER OF THOSE WHO WENT ASTRAY.

AMEN.

I say these prayers each morning and at night before I go to bed. I'm certain the Lord who created me hears my plea and won't let me die on the wrong path or lead me astray.

SEVEN YEARS OF BATTLING ADDICTION

I am your constant companion. I am your greatest helper or your heaviest burden. I will push you onward or drag you down to failure. I am completely at your command. Half of the things you do, you might just as well turn them over to me, and I will be able to do them quickly and correctly. I am easily managed.

You must merely be firm with me. Show me exactly how you want something done, and after a few lessons, I will do it automatically. I am the servant of all great men, as well as, sadly, all failures. Those who are failures, I have made failures; those who are great, I have made great.

I am not a machine, though I work with all the precision of a machine, plus the intelligence of a man. You may run me for a profit, or run me for ruin. It makes no difference to me. Take me, train me, be firm with me, and I will place the world at your feet. Be easy with me and I will destroy you. Who am I?

I AM A HABIT.

Dennis P. Kimbro is an author and motivational speaker.

There's a lot in my past I'm ashamed of. A lot of things I wish hadn't happened; some decisions I wish I hadn't made; some actions I wish I hadn't taken; some words I wish I could unsay; and, most importantly, some habits I wish I hadn't practiced, but they are now in my past. And if God has decided to keep me up till this day, then it is that God wants me to use my past as a window into a spotless future and not as a burden or an identity to be judged by.

A few years ago, I cultivated a deadly habit of self-pleasure, mostly known as masturbation.

I didn't initially feel guilty about defiling myself or, at the very least, ashamed of the immoral behavior. I thought I was instead being more cautious to avoid engaging in fornication. Being a male child going through puberty, I found myself overwhelmed with a strong urge for orgasm.

Suddenly, I started having unusual dreams, always involving myself and a lady in an intimate relationship. Most of the time, I don't recognize my partner, though occasionally it's someone I've earlier admired. When the dreams increased in frequency from twice per week to four times per week and then five times per week, I started to feel uneasy.

I was worried so much that I informed my mother of my situation. She sneered, saying it was the male kind of stuff. She added that at my age, I was expected to have such dreams. She did, however, urge me to keep an eye on my nutrition and to perform morning and dawn supplication (Du'a) before going to sleep.

Nothing changed or at least subsides as the weeks passed. Instead, it got worse because I started dreaming when taking a quick nap during the day and I still dream at night. I occasionally dream at noon that a woman entered my room and attempted to seduce me.

A few minutes later, I awaken to the coldness of the gooey fluid substance oozing from my lower organ.

Not just that, I also discovered that my ability to focus on a particular task and accomplish it was on the decline because my mind was preoccupied with sexual thoughts. I was losing my grip. I was losing my sanity. I was losing myself.

I became terrified. I brought up the same subject with my mother once more. This time, she identified with my feelings and then moved to act.

After telling my grandpa, who was still alive at the time, what I had told her, he sent down a one-liter plastic container filled with water and some traces of a brownish substance after three days. I was instructed to consume it twice—morning and night—along with a bath using the cover as a dosage.

I was relieved. It was over, and I became normal after three months.

Hold on a second!

This is where I would have loved to end this story. Allowing you to assume that the "magic water" of my grandfather healed me, but NO! There's more to this story. Besides, doing that would defeat and negate the purpose of this chapter and this book in its entirety.

I'm human. Just like you, I should also be aware that many questions will run through your mind, such as why on earth would any right-thinking person write a book and dedicate an entire chapter to admitting to being a sex addict who was healed by a supposedly magical mixture. **That's ridiculous! Isn't it?**

Nevertheless, please feel free to... think your thoughts.

Needless to say, I never would have published these lines if that was the motive behind taking up this awkward project. Moreover, time is too short and too precious to waste, and if I choose to waste mine, I've got better places to go waste it.

Some would argue that my situation was simply the result of an encounter with an ethereal being. Nothing could be further from the truth. I became more susceptible as a result of that practice and attracted to the invisible being (jinn).

Two months went by with consistent application of the "magic water" and vigorous bedtime supplication (Dua), but nothing subsided.

However, it is of utmost importance that I inform you that before the whole horrible girls' dream began, I was indulged in and committed to seeing porn clips and other pornographies. This may sound ridiculous, but you may be disappointed if the curtains fall off and you see how many people you know are victims of these immoral sites.

That is, by the way.

Let's continue.

At the time, all I needed was data and a charged smart phone to get the clips, but I never kept any of this on my phone. Like me, most victims don't either. I never knew or had any clue what damage I was doing to myself.

The Mirror Has All The Answers

But when the situation persisted, I had to summon the courage to look hard inside the mirror and say to myself, "I'm the problem."

You see, often I come across awesome, nice, and very positive-thinking people who are victims of these phonographic sites, and sadly enough, the numbers aren't decreasing. Many times I attempt to talk them out of it, but often they'll rebuke me furiously and claim they have no idea what I'm talking about.

All I try to tell people is that we are all guilty of one moral offence or the other, but this is no predicament (a situation nothing can be done about other than endurance), but a problem, and every problem has a solution, and if you let me, I can help.

I am not saying it's easy. I am saying it's worth it.

I guess you may be asking, "Do you go about asking people?" Common, I would be stupid to think anyone would open up to me about that immorality. However, if you are patient and attentive enough, I will reveal to you my tricks along the way.

Just be attentive!

The moment I started searching within... I came to realize that what I was doing was as good as committing mental sabotage... I was dying morally, psychologically, and spiritually all at the same time.

There have been a lot of contradictory views by experts in the US and around the world as to whether or not self-pleasure can deplete brain power or cause psychological complications. On religious and moral grounds, however, I choose to go with the former. Besides, why will I even take seriously a culture that preaches "polygamy is a sin while homosexuality is a right?"

Let's forge ahead.

The moment I was honest with myself by taking full responsibility for my ordeal, things began to change and solutions began to unfold petal by petal.

A Covenant with God

The first thing I did was to ask God for forgiveness and, secondly, for the spirit of perseverance as well as the mental toughness to commit to my new discipline. Then I struck a deal with God. Do this for me and I will do that for you. I resolved to never go back to it again. But I failed on the third day. I made a new resolve and failed on the 5th day. It continued in that sequence, improving continuously... This was how my journey started.

Now let me make a crucial note here.

The transformation didn't just happen because I had a covenant with God. It happened because in the course of my research I discovered that "habits are never eliminated, they are substituted." In other words, for you to get rid of a bad habit, you'll have to substitute it with a good habit.

I discovered something intriguing. I'm going to share it with you. Please pay attention. It's that important. What I found out is that with the help of algorithms or SEO (Search Engine Optimization), you'll continuously be getting content from sites congruent with your favorite site. If you're a football fan, you'll always get feeds on football news and other trending news. Those of you who are internet marketers know this for a fact.

Let me further explain this; if you are fond of watching porn clips on your device, whenever someone types in a keyword slightly similar to that which you're fond of entering, it will list all other related sites. For example, if the keyword you normally use is say, "XYZ.com" and for someone who wants to search for XYA, the moment he enters the first and second keyword, he will automatically see the list of Xs addresses you have previously entered.

Algorithms help platforms news feed you with similar content and also attract people of like minds to you. You may think it's a coincidence, but 'Nah' be rest assured, nothing is a coincidence about the internet.

I was following and liking various pages involved in posting nudes and other ill-content on all my social media handles.

When I discovered this, I began to delete, un-follow, un-friend, unlike, and wipe out my entire Google search history as well as every other suggestion related to this immoral content. The subscription I was using for those sites I converted into self-developing myself by watching YouTube videos on how to break a habit and stay disciplined and consistent, as well as how to develop successful habits and many more positive habits.

It is no lie that your identity emerges out of your habits and every action is a vote for the type of person you wish to become.

I committed my time to consuming self-help materials that would forever change my life. The books I stumbled upon are as follows:

- Atomic Habit by James Clear
- As a man Thinketh by James Allen.
- Awaken the Giant Within by Tony Robbins
- The Power of the Subconscious Mind by Joseph Murphy
- Effective Habits of Successful People by

Stephen Covey

All were in e-book format. So, it is easier to carry everywhere I go.

I would read at any slight chance until I consumed all the content, took note of every lesson, and applied religiously all the techniques I'd learned.

Some of the pearls of wisdom I gained and want to share with you are:

- The habits you cultivate will either make you or break you.
- I will be foolish if I strive to conquer the world, but I will be wise if I strive to conquer myself.
- I have learned to stand guard at the door of my ears because it leads way into my mind.
- I have learned to use my past as a window and not a mirror to be judged by.

PS: People get addicted to masturbation mostly due to the pornographic clips they frequently watch and because they watch it just before going to bed, which is then downloaded into their subconscious mind and stored, and anything that gets into the subconscious mind is difficult to eliminate.

PPS: Watching porn at any time is bad, but the worst is watching it at night before going to bed.

PPPS: Idleness is the fastest way to land you in a bad habit. Keep yourself engaged in productive activities, and if you are tired, take a nap.

WEIRD CHILDHOOD

I come from a family of nine and am the second of nine children. My father is married to two different wives, Zainab (my mother) and Maryam (my stepmother). There are currently 13 kids living with us, including four nephews, who are all in my father's custody.

Both mothers have their differences, but as the second and oldest son, I never let it affect or influence us.

Prior to moving into our own home three years after my stepmother joined our family, we spent our formative years in a neighborhood primarily populated by local farmers and traders. My mother, a medical professional who was frequently being transferred from one location to another, didn't spend a lot of time with us.

We practically grew up with our grandmother since our mother was mostly away at work. We were still very young when my grandmother joined us, and we lived together peacefully until her departure on February 28, 2021.My mum comes home every weekend and sometimes after 2 weeks. My dad made sure we never missed out on both Western and Islamic studies.

Three Demons

I had a weird childhood. We move in a clique of three. Paul, Hudu, and myself. We were referred to as the 3 demons. We were within the age range of 13, 14, and 13 years old, respectively, but we were a disaster. We committed a lot of atrocities at various locations in our territory and beyond.

We carry out every act together, but the idea often emanates from Hudu, who was a few months older and smarter than we were at that time. Any parent who criticizes us or shows any sign of resentment is putting his children as well as himself at risk of either being bullied or incurring property damage.

Though our parents were mostly away at

work, they made sure we were not left idle as we would close from western school, come home, take our lunch, and head straight to Islamic school until 5:30pm. Despite this tight schedule, we worked with our plan at heart, only searching for a careless two minutes to execute it.

I will quickly share only three stories from our weird childhood and then get to the lesson behind them each.

First story

I had a mistress in primary three who was quite cruel. Typically, she brings small packs of hibiscus beverages from home to sell. Because her product had an unpleasant taste, we didn't buy it. So we'll go out and buy it from someone else during break time.

She didn't make any sales the first day, so the second day she sent someone to keep an eye on what we were buying and where.

On the third day, right before break, she instructed everyone to get up and remain standing as though we had done something wrong. After that, she announced to the class who needed to make any purchases during the break time. Almost half the pupils raise their hands. She then asked that we place the money on the desk, which everyone did. I don't remember exactly how much I had, but since I was usually given two naira, I believe that's how much I put on my desk. She then instructed the class monitor—what we called "class reps" back then—to collect our money, distribute the beverage, and then give us the leftover change.

I cried bitterly. Times come and pass. After a year, the woman relocated into our neighborhood with her husband and two daughters. On seeing her, I recounted the ordeal, which I proceeded to update my friends about. The next morning, at around 9 a.m. or thereabout, we headed to her house just to survey what time they are usually at home and what time they go to work, as well as check if they had a dog or any form of security, etc.

Our plan was to go in and do some damage without leaving any trace. To cut the story short, we succeeded in carrying out the act. We broke into her apartment and broke two side mirrors of her husband's car in less than 60 seconds while her two daughters were watching a movie in the parlor.

We were later exposed after plotting the scheme with a snitch who never showed up. We received a heavenly thrashing from different people, including passers-by, and another badge of torment when my mum returned and was informed. I remained unchanged despite receiving all the penalties.

Second story

While still in primary school, another incident occurred. A classmate of mine had a womanizer for a father and was visiting a lady in my neighborhood. I went ahead to tell the son about the breaking news in the hope of receiving an accolade. Instead, he became enraged and began to fight me. Later, our mistress (who I later learned had passed away) called for us.

He gave a brief explanation of what transpired when she questioned the origin of our fight. I received heavy punishment and was treated harshly. But I was more focused on demonstrating my point.

It's Not Over Until I Win

I got home and started thinking about what I was going to do to prove my point. I called my crew and we brainstormed on what we were going to do. There was no cell phone at that time, so snapping was out of the equation. Finally, we came up with an idea. We were to use broken glass pieces to scribble our names on the car's burnet, where the boy could see them the next morning when he went to clean up the car. The three of us wrote our names, and the reason was that the boy knew we lived in the same neighborhood.

Let me save you these weird stories:

I could go on and on about even worse cases, like when we upgraded to using catapults to... and to using potash to evaporate locally made alcohol (Burukutu) at the boiling stage in the hope that the producers would run out of capital and thus close down the bar in the hope of aiding our friends whose parents were alcoholics, womanizers, and many other things...

However, the point I want to make here is that none of these severe punishments or torments had a positive impact on me. Maybe it did to some degree, no doubt.

Now, you may want to ask. Then what exactly changed you? Good question.

Third story

I do not remember exactly what class I was in at that time, but I was in secondary school, probably JSS1 or 2. One faithful Friday, my friend's parents had gone to attend the wedding of one of their friends. My friend came over and invited me to come and watch a movie. After an hour or so, the power goes off, and we remain in the parlor, hoping the light returns.

At the time, they had just bought a new color TV and we were still operating the black and white television set. Behold, the power came back, and since my friend wasn't close, I could not wait for him to come and put the TV on. I went ahead and put the switch on, and I heard a loud sound followed by a smell. My friend rushed in and got hold of me, screaming, "You have burnt it." You should have plugged it here. This is a stabilizer... But it was already too late. When his parents returned and discovered what had happened, he was vigorously punished but refused to say who was truly behind the damage.

It was during the weekend and my mum was around, so when she heard my father's friend threatening to hang him (his son) alive, she quickly called me and asked if I was aware or in any way involved in what he had been threatened with. I denied any knowledge of it. After severe torture, he gave in and opened up. My mother was later informed about it. She offered to pay for the damage but was resisted.

Within less than 48 hours after this incident, another of my friends came with breaking news about the discovery of an improved variety of mangoes being grown in one of the residences close to our Islamic school. We then plotted a plan on how we would break into the compound and pluck the fruit without leaving traces. After the plan was perfected, we then headed to the location, gaining access through the back.

The next thing we heard was the loud sound of gunfire, followed by a chase by two of his gatemen, but we both escaped separately. I came home scared that one of us had been shot. We were fully aware that it was a residence belonging to former commissioner of commerce and industry during military administration. At the time I'm writing these lines, it's been thirteen years since he passed on.

The Seven Magic Words That Cracked My Bones

Later on, the news got to my mother. That evening I didn't eat. Why would I? When I knew my days had come to an end. My mother was going to slaughter me tonight, I concluded.

One thing about my mother is that she never beat us in the daytime. It's usually at midnight when everyone has gone to bed. I went to bed waiting for my life to be taken, but to my greatest shock, nothing happened. The night went by without a single spank touching my body. I became confused. Something was just not normal, and I couldn't go out since I had not been punished.

I waited for my mother to act, but up until Monday morning she remained silent. My mum was in the sitting room getting her things in preparation for the trip back to work. I was also dressed in my school uniform, so I went in to pick up my school bag and headed out as there was no need to wait since I knew there was no way she would give me my weekly stipend after all I'd done.

Just before I stepped out, she mentioned my name, grabbed a chair and invited me over. She started towards the door and slammed it. My heart started pounding. She returned and sat just across from me.

Abdul, I'm your mother, she began. When I got married to your father, I prayed to God for children, and He gave me your sister. Later, I prayed more earnestly for a son, and God gave me you, along with your sisters. I carried each of you for nine months, enduring excruciating pain in various places, but I was determined to bring you into the world. With everything I had, I kept you safe. I breastfed you. I washed and changed your clothes until you could do it yourself. I did all that without anyone paying me to do it. I risked my life because I love you.

Now, if you are human, you can hear me and you can appreciate all my sacrifices... I don't ask that you pay me for the hardship I went through. I only ask that you don't be the reason I cry. I don't believe God wanted to punish me by sending you into my life. "Please don't be the reason I cry," she pleaded as tears streamed down from her eyes as she embraced me.

I've never again caused my mother to cry.

STAY YOUNG AND USEFUL

"You are only young once, and if you do it right, once is enough." (Joe E. Lewis)

You can't be an irresponsible, exploitative exploiter at the age of twenty-five if you want to be seen as a strong, trustworthy pillar of your community when you're fifty. The right time to worry about your reputation is before you have one.

There are only two ways that your story will be told after you leave this planet. Either as a warning or an inspiration. Being responsible while you're young increases your likelihood of developing knowledge as you come of age.

Making sure that your words and actions are consistent is the final step in accepting responsibility. Your usefulness, not your age, is what keeps you youthful. It's possible to be young at 70 and old at 20.

" If you want to be an old man for a long time, you must

become an old man in good time." — Marcus Aurelis

You can never make an impact in life by doing the wrong thing. It has never been wrong to do the right thing, and there has never been a proper way to do the wrong thing. Avoid wasting your life and being a burden on your parents and the others in your generation.

ATTITUDE MAKES THE DIFFERENCE

Permit me to tell you a short story. I attended one of the public universities in Nigeria. In my first year at university, I was allocated a bed space in a room of four (4) at the boy's hostel, but due to the magnanimous population, the room was later allocated to six students, making it a room of six (6). Five of the occupants brought in squatters each, which raised the number of occupants to 11.

The room became so crowded that four of the occupants would not sleep until everyone had taken their spot. Now, if I may ask you. All things being equal, what do you do if you find yourself in this situation?

Let me guess!

You're going to leave. Perhaps you will find somewhere much more conducive, more comfortable and more private.

There's no need for dialogue. That is what an average guy will suggest you do.

Right?

Well, for an odd guy like me, this is what I'll suggest you do instead: despite the disgusting situation, ignore all the inconveniences and focus on how to turn that predicament into a pleasant, enjoyable, and beneficial experience.

I actually did just that.

Please understand that I'm not, in any way or manner, trying to sound clever, smart, or egotistical. I'm merely attempting to explain to my readers the thinking pattern I employ each time I'm faced with an inevitable circumstance.

Because I couldn't change a thing about this unpleasant situation (in fact, I contributed to it), How? I had a squatter. Instead of complaining, whining, cursing, and hating as most people would do, I took a step back and asked. How can I benefit from this? How can I turn these disadvantages into an advantage?

It wasn't long before I figured out how.

In that room was a collection of three Yorubas (Lagos, Ibadan, and Kogi), two Hausas (Kano & Zaria), one Ebira (Kogi), and one Nupe (Niger), one Mumuye (Taraba), one Igbo (Rivers), and lastly, two Nasarawas.

With the right attitude, one can't imagine what a great potential learning opportunity lies in that room. These individuals represented a variety of cultures, ideologies, backgrounds, upbringings, perspectives, dialects, and, most importantly, personalities. My grasp of human nature and dynamism has improved as a result of studying these various qualities and ideals.

I saw people with awkward temperaments. People who are brave but envious, intelligent but dirty, aggressive but generous, polite but reckless...

"Everything is at your advantage if you view it through the right lens."—Abdul Shakur

Attitude is a difference-maker. Even if two people face the same obstacle or adversity, they will respond to it differently. One will turn out to be better than he was before the challenge, and the other will be bitter than he was before the challenge.

Let's say, for example, two fellows found themselves in a severe state of lack and starvation, but they differ in the lesson each one learns from that situation. One says, with what I've experienced during these hard times, I will never come across anyone in a similar situation, whether from my family or a total stranger, and not help him.

The second person says, with what I've experienced during this tough time and without anyone to help me, I long to see that unscrupulous element that will come and tell me he's my family and he's facing a major challenge and needs my help.

Same situation, same period, same place, but different lessons... Why? Attitude is a difference-maker.

Be A Good Student Of Life

It's not the magnitude of failure, obstacles, adversity, or misfortune that guarantees your success in life, but your attitude towards those misfortunes. We will always be at a disadvantage if we approach life as experts rather than as students. With the right attitude, you will turn scars to stars, misfortune into fortune, scarcity into abundance, and disadvantage into an advantage. You can't learn a thing if you won't accept that you don't already know everything. Learning doesn't just occur accidentally; learning must be intentional. What this means is that one must cultivate an intentional attitude to keep learning and growing through life.

People with a growth mindset approach each day with the attitude of "there's a lot I'm yet to know and everyone I meet has something I can learn from and every time I learn something I grow."

It will do us a lot of good if we stick to the advice of Donald Trump, which says, *"Stay young at heart."* We are given the opportunity to find a new center of gravity via challenges.

I believe that our attitudes account for more than 85% of our failures rather than our inherent intelligence. Learning requires more than just a sharp mind. It requires a big heart. Rarely does a scarcity mentality lead to abundance. Negative thinking rarely results in positive change.

Every day presents a fresh opportunity to learn something new. Everyone has something to teach me, and it pays more to listen than to speak if I want to learn and grow.

GOOD WISDOM COMES FROM GOOD LISTENING, NOT GOOD TALKING

"Wisdom is the reward you get for a lifetime of listening when you would have preferred to talk." — Doug Larson

You wouldn't need to be informed that I'm a natural talker if you had ever spent just a minute with me. Speaking comes more naturally to me than listening, but once I mastered listening, my growth began.

Talk is cheap. Everybody can talk, but you must develop good listening skills if you want to grow and succeed in life. In all honesty, if you are the only one speaking, you are not learning. After all, you lose nothing by becoming a student. To think you have all the answers means you don't know all the questions. It's wise to draw from your own experiences, but it's wiser to draw from the experiences of others.

While standing on your legs may not provide you with a clear view of a long distance, standing on the shoulders of others can. These are referred to as father figures, mentors, and teachers. Effective listeners hear not only what has been said but also what isn't being said.

Be a good listener. Take time to listen. It's no accident that we have one mouth and two ears. Listening is the best way to learn. If we must learn and grow fast, good listening is the key. When we fail to listen, we sure fail to learn.

THE COMMAND SAYS "Give!" NOT JUDGE

"It's not how much we give, but how much love we put into giving." —Mother Teresa

I want to put this question to you so you can answer it mentally.

- Have you ever tried to give something to a beggar and suddenly your mind jumps into scrutiny? Where you do find yourself probing if the beggar is worth the help, or if he should even be begging in the first place.

- After you're done probing this beggar, and you're satisfied that he "deserves" to be a beggar, what criteria do you use to "QUALIFY" who should beg and who shouldn't?

- Are you guilty of giving out food or other items to beggars mainly because they have gone bad and no longer hold value?

- Are you guilty of refusing to help the needy simply because you don't share the same faith? Or do you doubt if he's faking his amputation and so forth...?

- Having defeated all the negative voices in your head and having finally taken out money or any item to give to the needy, how do you reach out to them (from your standing posture)? Do you reach out to them like someone important or like someone irritating?

- Lastly, do you pick offense when you give out to a beggar and the beggar just takes the money or item and flees without gratitude?

Now, it's fascinating how Christian fellows quote Biblical scriptures like *"God makes the sun rise on the evil and the good and delivers rain to the just and the unjust,"* or the popular *"Do unto others as you would have them do unto you."*

On the other hand, Muslims cite a verse from the Qur'an that reads, "If you give alms openly, it is well; but if you do it secretly and give to the poor, it is better." "This will absolve you of some of your sins, and God is cognisant of all you do."

Yet each time we hear someone asking for help, we automatically become judges.

Is he a Muslim or a Christian?

Why can't he go and work like other people?

His amputation doesn't seem to appear real... so forth.

If you stick to the end, in one of the chapters I shared a life-changing personal experience I had with a beggar, and it might help you gain a new perspective on helping people.

Now, one more time, let me put these questions across so you can answer them for yourself.

Qs 1: Will you accept the offer if you are guaranteed a monthly salary income of N300,000 in exchange for giving up your dignity, such as sitting by the roadside without shade or any form of protection from the scorching sun, and asking passersby for assistance?

Qs 2: If you're guaranteed to receive N300,000

every month and the only task required of you is trekking 60 kilometres while carrying an empty plate and begging everyone you meet along the road for help (regardless of whether or not they give), you'll receive the amount promised at the end of the month. Will you honour this offer or recommend it to your son, daughter, or siblings?

Q3: Will you accept the offer to pick up your mother in a wheelbarrow and carry her into and around every corner of the bustling market place in your town for just 25 days each month in exchange for a guaranteed N300,000 each month? Or suggest it to your family and friends?

I'm not sure of your class or how much money you make each month, but I'm sure if you're a Nigerian and can afford this book, then you'll agree with me that a monthly salary income of N300,000 is a lot of money and that fewer than 30% of Nigerian employees receive this as a take home.

But I want to tell you, with a cold heart, that there are millions of Nigerians that will gladly take up all these offers you've declined for just a penny.

If your criteria for helping the needy is by examining their physique, what would you say about Hellen Keller, Zion Clark, Nick Vujicic, and Aaron Fotheringham...? How much would you recommend for this level of disability?

At the age of barely 19 months, Helen Adams Keller suffered a health problem that caused her to lose both her hearing and vision. Nevertheless, she went ahead and signed her name on the golden platter. She was the first deaf-blind person to complete a college education.

She was a nominee for the 1953 Nobel Peace Prize. In 1952, Keller travelled to the Middle East and met with regional authorities to promote the rights of people who are blind or disabled. This visit led to the nomination. Hellen grew up to become a household name as an author, political activist, and advocate for the rights of people with disabilities. She was also a "founder of the American Civil Liberties Union (ACLU).

Zion Clark was born with a medical condition named caudal regression syndrome, which means he was born without legs to his parents. On September 22, 2021, he officially became a Guinness World Record Holder after he broke the world record by walking 20 metres just using his hands. He completed the walk in 4.78 seconds.

Nick Vujicic was born without arms and legs but with two small feet, one of which had two toes. Nick decided to go into public speaking to inspire others. Nick founded his non-profit organization, "Life without Limbs," which gave him a platform to share his testimony and campaign against bullying. Since then, he has travelled to over sixty countries and inspired millions of people around the world.

Now, my friend, brother, sister, father, and mother, what can you make of this?

You'll attest to the fact that this has nothing to do with a lack of sufficient money. Rather, it has everything to do with mentality. This is a mindset problem. Why? Because, just as there are beggars in Africa, likewise, there are wretched beggars all over the continents: Europe, Asia, South America, North America, Antarctica, and Oceania.

If God didn't consult you before making you who you are or before giving you the parents, family, and privileges you enjoy today, please don't qualify people before offering to help them. The best way to appreciate God's favour on you is to not judge or qualify who he chooses to make king and who he chooses to make a servant of the king.

Please don't qualify people before offering to help them. The least you can do is wish them well and let them move ahead.

Never see people as a burden. Gain the ability to see beyond the obvious. Everybody has the potential to become something in life. Nobody was born in the lower class.

Make it your goal to make someone feel good about themselves because you crossed his or her path. After all, it is impossible to treat people well without feeling good about yourself. Remember, everybody in this world is searching for something, including the need for love, care, trust, understanding, recognition, companionship, respect, encouragement, and the desire to feel worthwhile.

Your hunger might not be for food, clothes, or shelter, but whatever it is, if you help many people achieve their desired goal, you'll eventually attain yours.

It's been said that we make a living by what we get, but we make a life by what we give. All of us are beggars in some sense. Besides, no one ever regrets being too helpful or too generous. Look for ways to give and contribute to uplifting others. The rewards are certain to come back to you in manifold and in many ways you'll never imagine.

The universal law states, " *The more of oneself and*

one's resources one gives away with no expectation of return, the more it will come back from the most unexpected sources and in the most remarkable ways."

Last but not least, if you've ever wondered why "God causes the sun to rise on the evil and the good, and why he sends rain on the just and the unjust," you might as well wonder why the vast majority of your gadgets, electronics, and automobiles are designed, created, and developed by people who don't even believe in the existence of the so-called God with whom you use those tools to praise and worship.

LESSONS IN THIS CHAPTER

- Learn to give without judging the recipient.
- Learn to assist others without expecting anything in return.

- When you assist someone, express your gratitude before they do.
- Treat people first-class.
- In the eyes of the Lord, we are all equal.

Whoever helps someone and expects something in return, however little it may be, is doing business, not charity.

"*The person who gives with a smile is the best giver because God loves a cheerful giver.*" —Mother Teresa

IT COST YOU NOTHING TO BE KIND

"Not everyone will appreciate what you do for them. You just have to figure out who's worth your kindness and who's just taking advantage of it. " – Unknown

The majority of people use two different sets of criteria for judging themselves versus others. We usually don't see ourselves as we see others. When we are given authority, we tend to be harder on our subjects than on ourselves. We become impatient with those we're giving power over.

We judge them according to their actions while judging ourselves by our intentions. When we make poor decisions, we are quick to rationalize by saying things like "nobody is perfect" or "you know what, there's a lot on my mind lately, that's why I did that." And then we let ourselves off the hook.

However, if the same mistake happens to others, we express dissatisfaction. We are quick to condemn. We complain. In other words, we forgive ourselves each time we're wrong but we prosecute others for making the same mistake.

PRESSURE CREATES A DIAMOND

In life, I have come to realize that things don't happen to us. Things happen for us, and our adversity is our greatest advantage.

In these trying times, the real us and the materials we're made of are exposed. Who we become depends on this moment. When a challenge is properly met, we emerge out of it wiser, stronger, and smarter; when it is not, we come out sad, miserable, broken, and shattered.

Before now, I've tried a lot of different things in pursuit of financial freedom. It all started in the second semester of my third year. At the time, life was hilarious. I was moving from debt to debt when I came up with a "no-fail formula" that sustained me throughout my stay at the university.

Under A Severe Challenge, The Mind Is Usually At Its Sharpest.

Before I continue, allow me to explain how my No-Fail Formula came to be. My parents were struggling and couldn't afford to send me my full monthly stipend. Even worse was that it wasn't month-end anymore but rather whenever they could afford to send me any amount and I'd have to manage it till they got money again.

Things were becoming increasingly difficult for me. I made the decision that if I was going to survive the storm, I would have to think of a source of income other than my parents because I was fully aware that I never had an uncle or other family member to turn to.

At the time, I had five close friends. I would borrow money from one of my five friends whenever I needed it, promising to pay it back within a week. In other words, if I take the money on Monday, I'll make up for it on the next Monday. If I don't get money from home by the sixth day, I borrow the same amount from my second friend to refund my first friend. If I still don't receive money within that week, I will go ahead and borrow from the third friend and go through the same process as the first.

While this may appear too simplistic to apply, there are 3 solid principles I adhered to that made it **"a No-Fail Formula."**

(1) I never forget when my repayment is due. That suggests I never allow anyone to remind me of the debt I owe him.

(2) I withdraw and remit money right away if I borrow it from someone and then receive it the next day from home. There have been instances where I borrowed money from someone that was meant to be paid back the following week, but I got an alert and returned the funds in as little as 30 minutes.

(3) This last principle is just as crucial as the first. Sometimes the lenders also borrow, and when this happens, I don't hesitate to lend out. If I don't have any, since I never have

spare cash, I go ahead and borrow from Mr. A and lend to Mr. B, and life continues... I want to assure you that I am still using this **NO FAIL** formula to date. You too can. However, I want to caution you that it takes discipline and character to sustain it.

If you never find a thing to learn in this book, at least this nugget is worth the investment.

Permit me to tell you about another fantastic technique I developed that helped me stay afloat. Before my final exam, I met Mr. Paul Obadiah, who just so happened to be my classmate. We became friends and since we weren't sure of graduating with our classmates, we were determine not to allow the outcome of the final result determine our progress in life. We will meet every two days to discuss issues relating to personal development.

A business strategy known as network marketing had already been discovered by Mr. Paul. Before that point, I was unaware of it. He told me about the company, and I went right away to look it up. I was pleased with the wealth creation vehicle and its ability to get me where I needed to go in life.

I was thrilled to discover a business strategy that I could use while attending classes. It's a business opportunity that will let me make money while I'm learning. Isn't it amazing? The only issue was that, in addition to being broke, I was also in debt, which further implied I couldn't afford the sign-up fee. I became obsessed with starting the business quickly and making some money. At the time, the enrollment cost was about N19,000 per person. And it is likely to rise at any time.

Time was moving faster, I grew more fixated, and I had just two days left with not even a kobo down for the sign-up. Suddenly, an idea crossed my mind. Why don't you use the wisdom you've acquired from the book "Power of the Subconscious Mind" to give your subconscious mind the task of figuring out how to get that sign-up fee? I immediately reached into my school bag and pulled out a blank piece of paper.

If you were with me and you saw what I was doing, you would think I had gone insane. But given the momentum and pressure I was under, it was not my first time doing it, and it has worked incredibly well for me in the past, so I knew this time wouldn't be any different.

I wrote, in uppercase letters, the following ten questions in succession with about equal spacing.

"HOW DO I MAKE TWENTY THOUSAND IN TWO DAYS?" ten rows at equal spacing. I'll read it as if I were delivering a fatal verdict or death sentence. Given that I only had 48 hours left, I made sure to read it at least 30 times every day.

Did it work for me?

Indeed, it did.

At the following day's nightfall, at around seven o'clock, Elijah and I were conversing as usual, but I wasn't paying attention because I was preoccupied with the question I had written earlier. When the answer finally dropped, I immediately stood up.

In disbelief, Elijah inquired as to what it was. I informed him that I was just going to demonstrate something and that I would explain it to him after I was finished. I instantly borrowed from the service provider because I didn't have any airtime. I went into my room and wrote down 20 names of people, some of whom I had never even asked for a favour, but whom I thought I might ask for assistance now.

I contacted them all and asked them to lend me each N3,000. Even though I only needed 19k, I went to bed that night with 27k in my account.

The good news is that even though I only asked for 3K from those who could afford to give me 10K, some of them sent 4K, 5K, 2K, and even 1K. And guess what? Most of the people who sent over 3K asked me to keep the money.

I'd like to make a point about this.

The solutions to this exercise don't come to you in the form of a whispered message or an audio message. They do, however, make themselves known through proposals or suggestions. They arrive in the form of "what-if information." "Why not?" and also "How about?"

Some of the propositions I received included, "What if you sell your Android phone and buy a button phone?" If you don't want to sell the phone, why not just give it to someone as collateral and collect N19,000? If that isn't cool with you, then what if you call Mr. A and ask him to lend you 20K to be repaid in 5 days? No, it seems a huge sum to risk and he might just decline with some excuses.

Alright! Then

What if you divide it into 5 separate places and tax 4 people since 4 x 5 equals 20? No, still enormous. What do you think of 3k from 15 people giving you 45k? That's good. After all, not all 15 individuals will give you the money. That's how I arrived at this. And if I still don't get the result I had expected, I will go ahead and explore other suggestions I had earlier declined to see if I can rework them better.

Now, let's continue with the chapter...

Where did I stop?

OK, life was so tough that I had to put my brainchild to work, and it did work. But this money I was borrowing was just to prevent me from dying of hunger and not to meet my other social needs (clothes, shoes, a new phone, and so forth). I decided to come up with a more productive idea. At the time, I had committed to personal development and had read two excellent books called "As a Man Thinketh" by James Allen and "The Power of the Subconscious Mind" by Joseph Murphy. I was now ready to start implementing the nuggets I took from those two books.

I took out a piece of paper and tried to brainstorm 10 ideas on how I could start earning money immediately after my second-semester examination since it's usually the longest break and incurs more expenses on resumption. I came up with roughly 16 ideas and struck out 11, leaving me with five solid ideas. Fortunately enough, the last idea manifested just days after I added it to my list.

It was suggested that I speak with one of my instructors, who I assume runs a high-income business in addition to his role as a lecturer due to his extravagant lifestyle, numerous cell phone engagements, and other factors. Since I had been observing him for some time, when

I tried to think of a way to escape my predicament, his thoughts crossed my mind. As God will have it.

Even before I finished my exam, the last option produced a result. When I went to say my 4 pm prayers, I ran into the lecturer I had intended to meet after my exam. Before he arrived, I had just finished washing, so I offered to get him water, to which he gestured.

I greeted him once we had completed praying, and he enquired if I was one of his students before asking for my name. He continued to inquire whether there were any problems, and I said not really, but I was going to come and see you in a few days. When he asked if I had finished my exams, I said that I still had one to write. He then told me he doesn't reside on campus and only comes around if he has classes. I then enquired as to his next scheduled appearance. He said Thursday, which was in two days and by which time my exam would be over.

Later, I ran into him in his office, and he asked me to have a seat. He asked why I wanted to see him. I'm one of your level 3 students, I began. Oh yes, I remember that face, and you seemed to always sit in the front row. He interrupted.

I continued. I'm facing severe financial challenges trying to keep up with my studies because I no longer receive the monthly stipend I usually get from home due to some challenges back home.

My parents are retired civil servants. I am the oldest of my parents' children, and I also have siblings. I sense that things are tough for my parents back at home, even though they have not mentioned it to me.

At the moment, I may not be buoyant enough to help them or even support my younger ones, but I wish to lessen the burden of paying my school fees when they're due. So that is why I have chosen not to return home but instead to stay back and put my hands to good use.

I want to work. Please help me.

MY FIRST JOB INTERVIEW

After listening to me, he appeared more humorous, and after a few seconds of deep thought, he asked. But why have you chosen to ask me for help? Or are there other colleagues you had planned to talk to too? Then I replied.

During the lecture period, you often excuse yourself to receive calls that sound more like business deals, and most of the time I overhear you negotiating prices and giving orders for a job to be executed.

In that light, I figured there's probably some other business you do other than what most of us know you for. Then he opened up and said, Well, you're right. I'm a contractor, and I carry out various contracts here and there. If you understand what that means, then I want to ask you, "What can you do for me?" In other words, what is your skill? What service can you render?

I was stunned and utterly lost in response to this inquiry. My mind wandered to too many other ideas. Considering things like,"You know, I have a diploma in electrical engineering, so I can change lamp holders, replace sockets, I wired my stepmother's battery cage, and so on."

I finally summoned the guts to admit—truthfully, sir—I lack any practical expertise, but I want to reassure you. I have two good arms—a healthy body and any task you give me, I will never disappoint you. At the time, I had my hair fully kept, and he jokingly said, "What if I ask you to supply cement at the building site, will you place it over your head?" Then I answered, sure! I will act without hesitation.

Finally, he said to me upfront, for two reasons: I do not have any jobs for you.

First, that I do not have any work going on right now, and we are in the latter stages of a project and are unsure of when the next one will be awarded.

Second, I'm not sure where I can fit you in even if I do obtain a job.

After a brief period of silence, he continued, "Well, let me call my architect to see if the final work is still in progress and to see if they can accommodate you." When the architect arrived, a call was made to the painter, who initially resisted but eventually gave in.

When questioned regarding his boys' wages and how much he could afford to pay me, he said he paid his boys the sum of N1,500 daily but said since I was going to do just any petty job, he was going to pay me N1,000. I got started. I had mentally planned how I was going to save N500 and leave on the remaining N500 daily. The following morning, I set off for the site, which cost me N400 in transport to and from for the first four days before I finally moved into the site along with other laborers.

But unfortunately, I never got a dime after 17 days of hard labor, and in addition, I lent him (the painter) some petty change each time he wanted to buy soft drinks or eat anything hawkers brought to the site.

After over two weeks of difficult tasks here and there, hoping that I would quit and run away, I disappointed him (the painter). On realizing that, somehow he began to like me so much that he entrusted me with his ATM card, and each time he needed money to send home to his family, he would call the contractor and tender his request. I would then go to the bank to confirm payment and then proceed to carry out the transaction, after which I would then write the balance on paper for him to keep since he wasn't receiving an alert due to some bank issues he was yet to rectify.

One day, they disagreed on how much he had received from the contractor as his part payment. The argument got so tough that he was about to abandon the site. I had to interfere because I had details of every transaction that had taken place within that period.

I called upon the architect and the painter so we could clarify the argument, which we later did, but I later found out the painter was not happy about that because he felt he had been cheated and was running at a loss as he had made the mistake of buying some materials hoping that the contractor would compensate him in the end, but unfortunately, the contractor refused to acknowledge it.

I attribute this to the reason he owed me my seventeen days' wages.

Let me spare you the remainder of the story and get to the end.

I was later absorbed by the contractor and given the office of storekeeper. He placed me on a monthly salary of N30,000 and occasionally gave me feeding allowances. He later paid my school fee for that year. I left after I received my second salary. Together with other savings, I returned to school with over N70,000 in my name.

Let me re-state it again.

WITH MY HARD-EARNED 70,000, I LEFT FOR SCHOOL

I returned to school a big boy.

Please understand that I have been in possession of three times that amount, but not from my sweat. All this time, I never told my father about my struggle, but I informed my mother about it on my second week with the painter. I only told my father I was staying back at school to study for my carryover courses, and he later sent me the monthly stipend I was using to feed myself while still working with the painter. He finally got a glimpse of my struggle when he called to ask how much he was going to send for my school fees and other expenses, and I told him all had been taken care of.

From that day on (after the interview), I learned never to approach anyone for assistance or help of any kind without an offer at the back of my mind. I approach people, no matter how influential they may be, with the mindset of a partnership, not a laborer's mentality. And that is because I came to realize that influential people don't like to welcome just anyone (who doesn't have any value to offer) into their affairs. For this reason, I don't take any learning opportunity lightly or perceive any skill as menial or unimportant. You might not know what will save you one day.

Let me share with you one more experience I gained during my six months of industrial training (IT), which usually took place in the

2nd semester of 400-level. I didn't know anyone in the city where I had secured my training other than one of my distant relatives. I went ahead to stay with her and her family. I was spending an average of N350 to and from on a daily basis, from where I was staying.

One day, she asked if there was any form of allowance given to us at the company I was training at, to which I responded, "No." She then decided to help me secure somewhere closer to the place I was conducting my training. After vigorous scouting, she finally found a place for me, and the following day I arrived.

This man is one of the kindest men I've ever met. He took me in and gave me one of the rooms in his boy's quarters. However, because he had five grown-up female children, he expressed some degree of reluctance to fully accommodate me for the remaining two months I had left. I sensed that, and of course, any dad will fight to protect his children, which I understood. I went ahead to stay, but I decided to never return home early, even though we were closed by 5 pm. I will hang around until 6:00 pm, then I will go into the house and straight to my room, take my bath, and go to bed.

A few weeks before I rounded up my training, I was already receiving food from his wife. I awoke one morning and went into the main flat to greet him when I heard him on the phone, asking someone to come over and iron his clothes because his housekeeper was nowhere near. So I immediately asked him to hand me the job. After some resistance, he finally let me take the job.

His wife later told me he was astonished when he saw the excellent job I had done. He said he had never seen such unique and excellent caftan ironing style ever before. From then on until I left, I never bought food ever again, and for your information, he has asked that I choose any of his daughters to marry if I please.

By the way, what brought about this bond, this

trust, and connection?

Probably not my English nor my degree. The man in question is a retired oil company employee who was enjoying his entitlements with not much to worry about. However, because I learned a skill, other people would rather term it a waste of time. And guess what, I learned this skill from one of my roommates in that congested, dirty, filthy, dilapidated room I stayed in while I was in year one.

A GIFT OF FAILURE

Adversity has helped me to discover my potential. If it wasn't for the adversity, I wouldn't have written this book. Just like every other graduate, I would have been doing the "Spray and Pray approach." You spray your curriculum vitae (CV) all over the ministries and organizations and pray that someone considers you.

Today, life is tough, but tomorrow it will be a lot tougher for those who go through it without growing through. You know you're on the right track for growth once things stop being easy. If it wasn't for the failure, I wouldn't have looked within. If it weren't for the experience I have gained, I would never have learned to value success no matter how big it may be.

If it weren't for the challenges, I wouldn't have discovered my potential. I can accomplish most things today because I was a force to stretch, exceeding the limits I once thought I couldn't reach. I have come to understand that there is no such thing as success by luck. Achievers typically don't rely on chance and instead define luck as being ready for an opportunity.

I've come to understand that, if we have the bravery to call it forth, whatever is genuinely within us or what we are made of emerges at the pivotal moment. Because I have fallen too many times, I have learned not just to stand back up but also to fall forward. I have also learned that it is better to prepare and not have an opportunity than for the opportunity to come and meet me unprepared. It is a fact that adversities don't make us who we are. Adversity merely reveals to us who we truly are. Your toughest times will turn you into the toughest person because what doesn't kill you surely makes you stronger.

If I had never faced the challenges I did, I

would never have discovered my potential. I never would have broken free of the limiting belief I've been left with for 27 years... If there's one thing that will never bore me, it will be the wisdom I gain from each experience.

Most people believe that life is supposed to be easy and hassle-free. They expect the government to solve all their problems and pay all their bills while they do nothing. Most people want to get the prize without paying the price. That's not life.

Challenges are what distinguish winners from losers, champions from failures, participants from spectators, and winners from victims. Without adversity, obstacles, or challenges, there would be no creativity, no transformation, and no advancement.

Problems are not to be mourned. Problems are to be solved, and all it requires is the proper use of the mind. A world void of problems is a graveyard, and no one wishes to leave there. The best time to grow is at the lowest moments, but you can only make the most of that moment when you're operating with the right attitude.

LET LIFE STING YOU FOR A LITTLE WHILE

Life is difficult and unfair. Only those who persist in life are rewarded. When you persevere and make a commitment to move forward despite obstacles, life will get weary of whipping you, and then comes a big break. It's OK to rest when you're tired, but never give up.

If at first you are unsuccessful, try again with a different strategy or a different approach. Keep at it. Develop a stone crusher's mentality and mental toughness, and one day your success will appear to have happened overnight.

Do not make quitting an option. Realize that challenges come at you constantly in life. For stars to shine, darkness must be present.

Your breakthrough is right around the corner if you don't give up, even when things are difficult. A person's perseverance in the face of obstacles and bad luck is a measure of their character.

Life becomes easy for people who are hard on life. And life becomes hard on people who are easy on life. Life is full of adversities, hassles, challenges... And most of the time, we do not choose what happens to us in life, but we can choose how we respond to what happens in our lives.

Anyone can become a male. The goal is to die as a man. Males are born. Men are made. You'll see me strive, you'll see my weaknesses, you'll see me down, but you'll never see me quite.

NEVER SHY AWAY FROM YOUR IDEAS

"Think big and beyond your lifetime if you wish to do great things."—Unknown

Don't undervalue the worth of your thoughts. Whatever the quality of the concept, if nothing is done with it, you will not benefit.

Ideas are gifts from the Creator to mankind. However, these ideas are not to be kept, they are to be acted upon. They were given to us so we could bring them to life. People walk around with a billion-dollar idea embedded in their head but are terrified or feel stupid enough to even say it to anyone.

Why? because they are afraid of being mocked.

Why? Because they're afraid it will fail if they dare to act on it and the world will make them a laughing stock.

Where would the world be if Graham Bell hadn't acted on his idea to invent the telephone?

Where would the world be if the Wright Brothers hadn't invented the airplane?

Where would the world be if Thomas Edison hadn't invented the light bulb?

God didn't create chairs or tables; he created trees.

God didn't create iron, metal, or steel; he created rocks.

God didn't create suits, T-shirts, jeans, etc. He created cotton.

People may not remember what you said you'd do, but they will never forget what you did.

Failure isn't so bad if it doesn't attack the heart. "Success is all right if it doesn't go to the head." RICE GRANTLAND

Tom Peters acknowledges, *"If silly things were not done, intelligent things would never happen."*

GOLDEN "A"

My first year at university was so tough. My heart was broken when I saw my first semester results. I decided I was going to quit the program because my performance was so terrible that my best grade was a "C" in English, my favorite course. I was discouraged and depressed, so I called my dad to inform him of my decision to return home because I was not going to make it in that atmosphere.

The first question my father asked me was, "Are you withdrawn?" Then I said no. Are you expelled? I replied, "No." So why do you want to come home? My result is too bad. I don’t want to waste your money here; this isn’t a place for me. I replied. My father gave me these uplifting words for the first time in my life: Abdul, if you still have faith in God and you believe that anything is possible with him, put your troubles aside, put your head down, and resume your studies.

By the way, have you forgotten how many people took the exam and how only a select few passed it? He continued. How many people submitted applications but only a select handful were accepted? God didn't bring you there to humiliate you. Ask him for assistance if you still have faith in him.

My second year came. We were to offer a course called "Engineering Drawing (MEEN201)." The first time I attended the course, I was shocked by the number of students offering the course.

So, I asked someone sitting beside me why there were too many people offering that course, including some intelligent guys I knew. And he said it's one of the most complex courses in engineering and most people not only carry it over, it prevents them from graduating. On hearing that, my heart started to race.

The lecture began, and I paid attention to avoid missing a thing, and interestingly, I comprehended each step...

When I returned to the hostel, I asked one of my roommates, who was a level higher but was also carrying over the course, to help me with the handbook containing worked examples. To my greatest surprise, I was able to get the concept, and not only was I able to comprehend the concept, I also went ahead to do some exercises.

In no time, people discovered me and I started receiving people from different departments and other faculties who were offering similar courses. As far as that course was concerned, I was a genius. I was consulted by smart and intelligent people for clarification, other troubles and many more... The exam came and I made an outstanding grade that we referred to as "A^{+}" (points greater than 70). And this was my first A grade, and it was my best A. Hence, I call it a "Golden A."

After that course, I continued to struggle with other courses. I put in the work and gave all the necessary attention, but I was still rolling on C, D, and Fs. Many times, I get mocked by my classmates who say I spend more time in the library than anybody but still battle with CDF.

I grew frustrated and started to wonder if there was anything wrong with me. I could simply cram the formulas and solutions, like most people do, but something inside of me wouldn't allow that. I detested numbers, but I needed to comprehend this course. I'm that person who will fill an entire booklet with theories while ignoring the most basic math. Often people will ask me questions like "Abdul, Why engineering???"

A GOOD COMPANY IS PRICELESS

"*Not all diamonds come from earth. There are those from the womb.* "—Abdul Shakur

Mark Twain put it best, "*Keep away from people who try to belittle your ambitions." Small people always do that, but great ones make you feel that you, too, can become great.* "

My story will never be complete without bringing into light some special people I met along my journey. It was a humbling blessing for me to have met such special people. When I first met Elijah, I was in my senior year. He had just finished moving into the complex where I was residing. I went over to him and struck up a conversation with him about life in college and then life beyond college because I'm constantly on the lookout for people of like mind.

I quickly realized he had resources I could draw from. He was a genius in both mathematics and other subjects, and since I had always struggled in math classes, Even though I was a level higher than him—level 5 compared to level 3—I knew there was a lot I could learn from him.

We were very similar in many ways. Things like a strong desire to better oneself, to amass wealth, or to improve one's spiritual life. We became so close because of our shared goals, to the point where two of the other tenants asked me why I had suddenly accepted a stranger into my life while keeping a distance from them. I didn't feel the need to explain myself at the time because I thought it would harm the relationship more than help it. I only sought for their understanding and supported it with the math lessons I was learning from the so-called stranger.

You see, Elijah is one of the three people who, earlier on, saw something in me when I couldn't see it in myself. Naturally, I'm a people person, of course. Therefore, anytime I meet someone, I tell them about myself, including things I admire, hate, and despise. I make an effort to be receptive to others, and I believe that my approach inspires others to replicate it.

And doing just that helps me know, without wasting much of my time, if you are someone I can hang around with. I'm interested in learning about your philosophy, ideology, belief, perception, and thinking pattern. So, to get a clue of who I'm dealing with, I entice people to speak about their dreams, goals, ambitions, and desires—as well as their fears and worries.

We would talk for hours about our experiences, good, horrible, and ugly. Additionally, he would listen carefully to whatever I said because he has a good listening attitude. When I'm done, he frequently draws attention to anything I mentioned that he found interesting or useful, and the same is true for me.

But Abdul, if you say you're not intelligent, I get confused if you're talking about someone else. He will often say, even if you struggle with math, you are still brilliant. Perhaps you're not a school kind of person, but when you speak, I can tell that you have great potential for success. I've only seen a few people with this gift so far. Many concepts that I previously believed I understood are now clearer to me after hearing you explain them. For instance, I've been familiar with network marketing for more than ten years thanks to my father, who joined the company when they first came to my state but decided I should represent him at training so I could better explain the business model to him.

I terminated my training after he passed away. In your case, it's just been two weeks since you joined this company, but the way you explain the business is so clear and alluring that I'm starting to wonder if I had hung on to it, maybe I would have been swimming in millions today.

What am I trying to say here?

Elijah didn't perceive me as I was, he perceived me as I may be. He saw gold in me when I could only see bronze and silver. I must confess that he is the motivator behind publishing these lines...

If he had not told me that my story was inspiring and educative, I wouldn't have thought of immortalizing my experience. I would have taken it with me to my grave.

As the great orator Myles Munroe asserts, "The wealthiest spot on this planet is not the oil fields of Iraq or Saudi Arabia. Neither is it the gold and diamond mines of South Africa, the uranium mines of the Soviet Union, or the silver mines of Africa. Though it may surprise you, the richest deposits on our planet lie just a few blocks from your house. They rest in your local cemetery or graveyard."

The second person I'd love to credit my achievement to is Mommy Favour. I had just joined network marketing, involved with health products known as supplements, and had set out for product sharing (selling of products). I was basically checking into offices and making a presentation when I landed in her office.

The office was occupied by three staff, and at the time I checked in, there were just two of them. I made my presentation and asked if they could try out my product, which they both declined, but just before I took my leave, Mommy Favor asked if I had a product that could relieve her migraines. I told her I did have another product that would help.

I took out the product alongside a liquid used for tooth brushing and handed the items and my phone number to her while collecting my money. I had this sense that she didn't need the product but just an act of kindness and encouragement. She called me the next morning and asked me to bring my products with me to her office so I could promote them to her coworkers there. I swiftly made my way to the office from the lobby. In just that one office, I made a ton of sales.

It was clear that Mommy Favor just wanted to encourage me as she was moved by my choice to work for independence. I thanked her and, just before I left, she asked if I could help her get a glaucoma product even though she already had a doctor taking care of her predicament. She insisted on patronizing me further. I provided her with a list of the products she required, but I also suggested the best product out of the other five since she could not afford all of them at once.

She asked me to place an order, and when the order arrived, I delivered it to her residence using the address she had provided. She pulled out some cash and inquired about my expenses, including my transportation costs, to which I replied. But she asked right before she gave me the cash. Do you really think this will work for me? And have you ever given it to any of your customers?

I responded to the first question by saying that I have implicit faith in the product of my company and that millions of people throughout the world have attested to its efficacy.

I replied to the second question, "I have never given it to anyone, and I have never used it myself." That is why I like you. Isa, she exclaimed.

Now, I'm saddened to inform you that the product in question didn't serve her well. Every evening I'd call to hear from her, and she would tell me she was getting better until she was drastically ill and couldn't go to work. She later learned from her doctor that the new health product, which her body had a difficult time adjusting to, was what had caused her abrupt illness and was urged to stop using it. Later, when I went to check on her in her office, I learned about her illness.

I went to her house, met her, and was heartbroken after examining her situation. I was taken aback when she said, "Isa" (she mentioned me by my surname). You see, there is no question that this stuff works. Because it didn't work for me, doesn't mean it won't work for others. I want you to take it, find a deserving recipient, and either give it away or, if you can, sell it. You seem to be different; you are honest and hardworking, and I encourage you to keep it up. You are going to be great someday.

I later called her to tell her I couldn't find

someone to give it to (not truly that I couldn't find someone, but I was nervous not to experience the same predicament), and has decided to use it myself. So I told her I was going home and wanted her account details so I could make some refund since she didn't even take up to half of the product, but I never got the account details. Instead, I got this message.

"Thanks so much for your effort. Whatever you do is okay by me. I pray God will prosper any steps you take in Jesus' Mighty name, Amen. Take care and I wish you merciful travels. "

And ever since, we communicate every now and then. I have also been receiving her texts urging me to persist in my struggle and also reminding me that if I never relent on my effort, I will be a success. This encouragement has kept me growing through adversity after adversity.

The third person that has impacted my life is a guy called Mr. Paul Obadiah. Obadiah was my course mate, and our lane crossed when we were just about to round up our program (Part 5). I had just finished reading in the library and was heading back to my apartment when we met and exchanged greetings. He was holding a book authored by Brian Tracy.

Seeing that, I thought I should be able to learn something from this person. And when I asked if I might borrow his book for a few days, he declined, claiming he had just bought it and intended to finish it by the weekend. I request that we have some time to talk about life's issues.

He gave his approval, and we scheduled a meeting. We later became very close, and he suggested a business plan to me. After doing my research, I registered under him as a new distributor. Even though I quit the business after a year and a half (the reason for quitting will be narrated in my business book coming soon). I can't deny how much of an impact that had on me, though. Especially in the areas of developing one's confidence, dealing with rejection, health education, public speaking, and, finally, leadership development skills.

Mr. Obadiah will continually compliment my leadership abilities and my capacity to successfully persuade my subordinates to take amazing actions and produce wonderful results whether or not I'm present. He never fails to call and praise my greatness.

LIGHT YOUR CANDLE

You can never shine trying to sit on someone else's sun. God will never give you what someone else is supposed to have. If you don't discover yourself, you can never take charge of yourself. The pressures of life test the reality of our gifts. Whatever stops us is how strong we are.

As Joyce Mayer observed, *"God will help you be who you can be, but he will never let you be successful at becoming someone else."*

To survive and thrive in this turbulent economy, you must constantly explore your gifts and potential. The majority of people attempt to follow the identity and way of life of someone else while ignoring their path.

They engage in activities that don't give them

satisfaction. Advancing another person's concepts and goals while ignoring their own. They disregard their talent, capacity, significance, or individuality.

Fish don't go to swimming lessons. But fish never have trouble swimming.

Birds don't go to flying academies. But birds don't have any trouble flying.

Barking schools are not attended by dogs. Dogs do not, however, struggle to bark.

Since talents are not learned but rather discovered, none of these creatures struggle to apply their gifts. Your gift is connected to your gold. Your potential determines your earnings, and your talent is connected to your treasure.

Your entire life will be filled with difficulty if you never find your gift, your potential, or your purpose. Why? You're attempting to soak up someone else's sunlight.

Don't die a duck when you were born an eagle.

DEFY THE STATUS QUO

"Everything is within your reach. You only need to stretch. "- Abdul Shakur

I was born into a mediocre family. I was not allowed to dream wild dreams. I grew up with pretty low self-esteem as a kid, and I lived with it until I was 27. It all started when I turned 15. Feelings of inferiority are something my parents unconsciously ingrained inside of me.

My father had a short temper and was always scolding, nagging, spanking, and shaming me all the time, not caring if I was just a child. All of these things were not unconnected to the trouble I'd caused him in the past, and even though I was a repentant son trying to be the best son I could be, he couldn't care less or even acknowledge my changed behavior.

This leads to my perfectionism. I won't attempt to do anything for fear it won't be perfect.

There was always this voice in my head that would talk me out of everything new I attempted to do.

- I can’t get it right.
- I’m not as smart as other kids.
- Wait until someone else does it.
- How would you be the first to spot an error in that exercise when all the gurus in the class couldn’t see it?
- Why don’t you do it just like everyone else?
- Why do you think it shouldn't be like this when everyone thinks it's best that way?

- How am I going to be the first person to go against the status quo of not doing the traditional thing?

The worst one is when I hear:

- Don't you think the reason you're at the bottom of the class is that you think differently from everyone else?

My inner fire was extinguished by these voices in my head, and as a result, I was unable to realize my potential until much later in life.

I went from being an adventurous kid to feeling timid, unfortunate, rejected, inadequate, and unworthy.

Each time I learned that the exam timetable had been released, I became terrified. When I get close to the exam hall, my mind will start to ponder over all sorts of questions;

What will the questions look like?

Will I even be able to answer the question perfectly?

What if I couldn't comprehend what the question was asking? And so forth.

I've always been terrified of failing, and failure is all I ever get.

I lived this way most of my life, thinking in terms of lack and hardship rather than abundance, until a few years ago. I break free and everything starts to change rapidly.

Most of the time, I'll smack an idea even before it lands for the fear that people will think I'm insane for having such a weird thought, only to see that idea brought to life by someone else.

On the other hand, my mother will constantly remind me of our financial difficulties and the need for me to avoid problems at all times.

Now, aside from her customary last sentence, "You know, we are poor. We can't afford to pay for damage of any sort." I never had any issues following my mother's counsel. Besides, I couldn't figure out why she said that all the time. It wasn't like we were that wretched. We fed well and never skipped a meal. We had nice clothes in our wardrobe that we occasionally gave out to the less privileged. We attended the same school as other fortunate kids.

Because she repeated that statement countless times, especially when someone came home to report me for something I had done wrong. I was conditioned to think in terms of lack rather than abundance. This feeling is also not unconnected with the realization that I'm low on IQ.

I strive to improve my self-esteem. I worked on my ability. I defy the status quo. I broke free!!!

For whatever reason, society wants us to believe that success requires a high IQ. They lead us to believe that in order to succeed, we must be literate, achieve high academic standing, or hold a degree. The brutal truth is none of that will be necessary if we can develop high emotional quotient, or EQ.

Since there was not much I could do about my Intelligence Quotient (IQ), I learned to develop and improve my EQ (Emotional Quotient). Contrary to IQ, practically everyone can have a high EQ, which is a wonderful trait. You only need to be aware it exists.

The ability to maintain emotional control no matter what happens is what you need to have a high EQ. A high EQ enables you to learn from your mistakes more quickly, make wiser choices when faced with difficult choices, and improve as a leader.

Being more empathic, self-aware, understanding others, and emotionally intelligent all go hand in hand with having higher EQ.

You are in charge of everything here. Because you won't be deterred by rejection, criticism, or failure if you have a high EQ, you will have a far better chance of reaching your goals.

LOSERS CAN'T DEFINE WHO YOU ARE

You're a champion. You're born for impact. You are a fighter, a survivor. You're a conqueror. You are out to make a difference and become a reference. A loser cannot define who you are. You came to this world a champion, having defeated 60 million opponents (sperm cells).

Those who tell you, "You can't," will come to celebrate your victory. If the earth didn't need you, heaven wouldn't have sent you. You belong to the class of winners. You are a dreamer and an achiever. You were not created to be ordinary. You didn't come to this world to be average. Never let a loser tell you who you are.

Dream big. Think your thoughts. Don't settle for less than life can offer you. You are destined to do great things. No one's opinion of you can cancel your destiny.

"Whether you think you can or you think you can't. You are right."- Henry Ford

RESENTMENT IS THE ATTRIBUTE OF THE WEAK

Never harbor resentment toward anyone. You never know who will be there for you the next day.

I once had a lecturer that I hated with a passion due to the terrible experience I had with him my first week at the institution. I resumed school to begin registration and other processes because I was new and naive. I couldn't accomplish anything by myself because, as I've already mentioned, I was worried that I'd make a mistake that couldn't be undone.

After paying my school fees and other dues, I headed to the department for signing and other documentation. On arrival, I was directed by another student into the coordinator's office. I entered and followed a cue, following which he requested that we wait outside before entering one at a time. When it was my turn, I entered the office and handed the man my green file. He quickly spotted an error in the list of my course outline, quickly packed up my file, and asked me to go make adjustments.

Because I was new, I didn't even know the precise courses I was supposed to offer and which I wasn't. In addition, the individual who filled mine was the same person who filled it for others.

In spite of being stranded, I was returning to campus from my department, Agriculture and Bio-resources Engineering, which was located 5 kilometers away. The weather was hot and dry, and it was the dry season. Even though I was depressed, I went to the campus for the changes, and once they were accomplished, I returned to the department. When I arrived, there was a fresh cue of about 15 students, and I quickly joined.

After about 30 minutes of waiting, it was my turn again, so I entered and handed the man my file. He quickly glanced through, and the next thing I saw was my credentials being flung into the air and asking me to get lost. I gathered up all of the papers and stumbled out, shattered.

While hunting for the office to turn in her file, I ran into a girl who would eventually become my course mate as I was leaving the building. She questioned if I had taken my file for signature. I explained to her that I hadn't because I needed to make some adjustments. She asked if I could assist in determining what change she needed to make. I informed her that I didn't know any better and that it would have been better if she had let him explain them to her on his own.

The course combination I saw in her course form made me feel sorry for her, so I chose to save my tears for her while imagining the details of her case. She pleaded with me to wait for her so that we could return to campus together for the correction.

She later returned to apologise for keeping me

waiting and further stated that she didn't have to come with me any longer because he had assisted her in making the modification using his computer and had also provided a complimentary reprint of her slip. Throughout my stay at the university, I detested him.

The second tale is going to be brief. This is another man whom I very much respected and held in high esteem. I looked up to him as a mentor and shared his joys and sorrows. To me, he was exactly like a parent. He had been there for me right up until the end. I had improved when my first semester level 5 results were out. I had already resolved to do my best work and graduate with a second class lower. Even though he was one of the examiners, I still wanted to hear his view, so after the results were announced, I went to obtain the transcript to show him. I approached him while approaching his office from the mosque and told him I had collected my transcript. I then pulled it out and gave it to him.

While he was glancing through my results, I

said. Sir, I hope I achieve my sole goal of graduating in second place. But do you think I can do it? In an instant, he replied. You can't. Your result has just improved simply because of the A you got here and there, or else it wouldn't have made any significant change.

I was shattered.

Surprisingly, this book has made it to life because of the motivation I got from the person whom I have hated all this while. And if he never gets to read this book, he will still never know how or in what way or manner he has influenced and motivated me to compile these pieces.

THE TOUCH OF CHRIST

I had been dreaming for quite some time that I would write my book someday. I met some amazing people who immediately raised my spirits, ignite my soul. My classmate Paul, who had persuaded me to join network marketing, was the first. He will always mention that he sees a fantastic leader emerge after a few months in the company. I had a few downlines at the time, and he could see that I was genuinely interested in helping them, and I was making many other significant sacrifices to keep them working toward a better future.

Mr. Paul will usually text me to thank me for what I did. The cost of their transportation, transporting my subordinates to the training, and the fact that some of them were experiencing severe challenges from their parents and other family members.

The second person is Elijah, whom I spoke of earlier in the previous chapter. and. The third person is Mommy Favour, also spoken of in the previous chapter.

Because I failed most of the core courses, I was forced to look elsewhere for a solution, and that is because I came to convince myself that God doesn't create failure. We are literally a success gone bad (the result of misplaced priority.)

There are just two reasons that have influenced the title of this book.

Firstly, the three awesome Christians that have motivated and elevated my spirit and vitality into realization and the awakening of the sleeping giant inside of me are Christian faithful.

The second reason has been that virtually 90% of the personal development books and materials I stumbled on that have helped transform my life have been written mostly by pastors and bishops. Hence, the title "The Touch of Christ."

IT'S NOT TIT FOR TAT

One of the crucial lessons I learned earlier in life was to never take vengeance for evil deeds. For quite some time now, I've tried to recall who tossed this philosophy into my mind since I was a child and has made it stick firmly to my heart.

Despite all the effort put into deep recollection, I still couldn't remember who, where, and what took place at that moment. Yes, I could, but I refuse to make up stories for it.

However, what I still recall is someone saying to me or perhaps telling another kid, "Never take vengeance if you've ever been wronged." Remember, not everyone was lucky enough to have a mum like yours. "

This one lesson was a life changer for me. I've been trying for a while to remember who first introduced me to this awesome philosophy as a child and how it managed to ingrain itself so deeply into my being. Despite my best efforts, I was still unable to recall who, where, or what happened at that precise moment.

But the phrase, "Remember that not everyone was lucky to have a good mother like yours." is something I can still clearly remember someone saying to me or possibly telling another child

I've always wondered how impactful this message has been on me. I have always credited my resilience to this philosophy. Whoever did this to me, I pray that God will reward him or her wherever he or she may be. I grew up with this message held close to my heart, yet I don't know who, where, or what took place that led to this powerful insight. I have been living by this philosophy for as long as I can recall.

This philosophy has helped me approach tough situations from a point of strength rather than weakness.

Someone said, "Whoever triggers your emotion has your control." Nothing could be further from the truth. Until recently, while listening to the lectures on "The Life of Jesus," someone helped me reiterate this viewpoint.

When he (Jesus) preaches the word of God, people will curse him. When he tells them what God forbids them, they will throw stones at him and many other harmful objects. But while they were pouring curses at him, he was pouring blessings at them.

Someone who found that attitude ridiculous approached him (Jesus) and said, "Hey you," Despite the hatred and abuse you receive from these people, you continue to send them blessings. What's the reason for that? Jesus replied, "They are sending what they have, but I don't have that which they have, so I will send back what I have."

Forgive people not because they deserve it. But because you don't deserve to be trapped in the past.

Unless you too have evil, you can't avenge an evil act. You can't give what you don't have.

DREAM SABOTEURS

It is self-deceptive to think you can keep the company of negative-minded people and have a positive life. Make no mistake: The company you keep will undoubtedly influence your results in life. There is no such thing as casual friendships. Whoever is not adding value to your life is taking value out of your life and that person is a liability to you because a liability is one who doesn't add to your abilities. It is preferable to be alone than to be in bad company.

We are unavoidably impacted by those around us. It is almost impossible to alter your life without first, changing the people in it.

Some people are excellent dream killers. They'll talk you out of your dream the moment you mention it. They steal and destroy your dreams and blur your vision. Rather than encouraging you, they bring discouragement, fear, and hopelessness. They take away your confidence.

These are people who have concluded they can't be successful in life because no one in their family or generation has ever amounted to or achieved anything significant in life. These types of people need to be discarded because they can make your journey stressful, thus hindering you from enjoying your ride to your destiny.

They will make every effort to talk you out of your dream. They will go as far as to tell you. What we're doing now is what we inherited from our parents and their parents, and it's what has kept us going to this day. And now you, a child of yesterday who has broken with tradition, have come to tell us you've found a better way of life by doing things nobody here has done before. And so forth.

If, after all of this, they are still unable to persuade you to give up on your dream and lead a normal life like every other person, they feel disrespected, disregarded, or even challenged.

Sometimes it could be frustrating and you'll feel broken and demoralised and you'll be saying to yourself, "Why can't they see that I'm not doing this for me?" I'm doing this for the entire family. " But no, all they see is that helpless tiny creature that was born a few years ago and now tells them he can do what they couldn't.

These are people who are going nowhere and want others to stagnate with them. So when they see you heading toward greatness, they feel threatened, intimidated, frustrated, and restless. Why? Because if you succeed, they will be declared a failure.

You'll be disappointed to learn that 80% of these people are among your family members, 15% are friends, and 5% are strangers. In most cases, these people think they are trying to help you, protect you, and guide you in their way. This is not what you need. What you need is support, encouragement, and prayers.

In dealing with humans, it is important to understand that people can only comprehend at the level of their perception. You are not responsible for making sure people understand you. Making sure you understand yourself is your responsibility. If you did not emanate from a rich family, a rich family should have emanated from you. Because a rich man is no other than a poor man who has gotten tired of being broke. Some people come into your life to strangle and suffocate your goals and dreams. Beware of such people and keep them as far away as possible.

It is certain that people will criticise you once they see you begin pursuing your goals and striving for excellence. So you might as well get accustomed to it and grow an alligator skin. However, it's important to avoid internalizing it. Don't let it get the best part of you.

I'm of the opinion that the best place to chase your dream is outside your comfort zone. Go somewhere where no one or very few people know you, then start hustling and working your way up the ladder of success. Whatever chokes off your ideas, suffocates your initiatives, squashes your thoughts or stifles innovation must be avoided at all costs. Take every precaution to prevent anything that impedes your development, physically, psychologically, or spiritually.

Go for people who will promote and sell you, not those who will bring you ruin, reproach, and shame. Greatness comes with a price. Superiority has a cost. You must be willing to lose some friendships. You must be willing to be misunderstood. You must be willing to experience hatred, neglect, insults, disdain, abuse, and disrespect if you want to reach the top.

CAPITALISE ON YOUR MISTAKES

"The difference between greatness and mediocrity is often how an individual views a mistake." —NELSON BOSWELL

It is believed that anyone who makes a mistake but never capitalises on it has made bigger mistake. Why? Because each mistake serves as a revenue for your future investment.

Everyone experiences failure in life, but how each individual views failure determines whether they are a successful or mediocre person. While one sees failure as an event, the other sees failure as an identity.

One failed and prayed "God forbid I fail again". The other failed and praised God, saying, "I've found one sure way that this idea won't work."

One sees failure as a learning opportunity, the other sees failure as a curse.

One views failure as a requirement for achievement, whereas the other views it as a barrier to success.

One fails and gains knowledge, while the other fails and muses.

Berthold Brecht put it best, *"Intelligence is not to make mistakes." But to quickly see how to make them good."*

It is ok to accept failure. Cry if you have to but don't just stick it to heart.

There is always a cost involved in moving forward, and the amount you refuse to pay today will be paid tomorrow with interest.

Never be afraid to try a step if you are sure it is the right one.

FAILURE REDEFINED

How does it sound to hear the phrase, "You are a failure"?

Isn't it a terrible thing to say? But the query I would like you to pose is: Success in achieving my goal, or success in achieving yours?

What most people consider a failure actually isn't?

For a better understanding, let's make an illustration here. Two young Igbo men decided to open a business in the northern region of Nigeria. They realised that in order for their venture to succeed, they would need to learn to communicate with the locals in their native tongue.

They both made the decision to reapply to secondary school and take all nine subjects from scratch (Hausa language included).

After a number of years, they took final exams in all nine (9) subjects. When the results were out, the first student earned eight (8) "A^{s}" in all other subjects but got an "F" in the Hausa language. The second student earned eight (8) "F^{s}" in all other subjects but got an "A" in the Hausa language.

Which of these two men is considered a "failure?"

The second student will be perceived as a failure in the conventional sense, I suppose. But is he really?

However, a clever man knows that the individual with eight (8) “A^{s}" has blundered.

Let's examine a different scenario. The area where my family's home resides is faced with the challenge of a lack of drainage system. Water just flows by gravity into every possible location for that. Unfortunately, the surface runoff logs in at an apartment building behind our building. Every attempt to avoid water logging in that area was unsuccessful. Meanwhile, a plot of land just next to this building is flooded, and the owner of that plot plans to launch a project there.

Having seen the state of the place, he made a cunning decision. He appealed to the locals there to contribute to the construction of a drainage system that would collect runoff and reroute it into the drainage system leading down to the stream. Those of you who reside in the remote area should know what the outcome of this meeting will be. Very few people were willing to invest money in this initiative, and the majority said that the government should handle it instead.

This "clever" man pinpointed the exact location of the strong flow and marked the spot, creating a drainage system across the area where the water will enter and exit. This drainage system runs along my fence and through my gate, making it impossible for my father's car to move out for two good months.

The walls were built using 6" blocks, and they extended just past our gate, abandoning the remaining 220 metres of earth wall drainage that, if not cemented, will eventually cause our fence to collapse. This episode drew a lot of outrage and criticism, as well as insults and all kinds of foul language. I never wanted to speak up, though, for only two reasons:

(1) I wasn't present when the whole dialogue took place. And

(2) Whining and ruminating on the problem never solves it.

Once I sense that the participants in a conversation are unwilling to hear the truth, the facts, or the wisdom of experience, I typically avoid interjecting. A few others who were interested in learning were around, so I decided to jump in. I questioned the man whose phrase "he's a failure" I overheard. I queried, "Why did you term him a failure?" because he had earlier claimed to have taken up and completed numerous capital projects in major cities. He replied.

But what if I tell you that expression is inappropriate in this situation? In my opinion, if we take a close look at it. The first inquiry is: what was the justification for the project's execution, and was it met?

I don't know what his intentions were, but if I were to infer anything from what happened, I would say that initially he intended to find a solution to the issue as a group, but when the populace refused, insisting that it wasn't their issue, he made the decision to find a solution to his issue while letting them find a solution to theirs. The man who completed the job may be considered a failure by others, but to himself (having resolved the water logging problem), he is a success.

That is, by the way...

The point I'm trying to put across is that "no one" is qualified to call you a failure other than yourself. In other words, failure is subjective rather than objective.

Besides, if we begin to view mistakes through the eyes of a statistician or scientist, we will stop seeing failure as a bad thing. In science, mistakes precede discoveries. A mistake for a scientist is not a failure, but rather feedback. It is known as a hypothesis by statisticians. They are able to understand what has happened by using this outcome, as well as why it has happened and how it happened.

From my perspective, anyone who succeeds in failing at any endeavour should be celebrated, if not awarded. Why? People wouldn't have to go through a failed system or practice since he has correctly identified one surefire way an idea wouldn't work. Therefore, it is important to say unequivocally that no endeavor devoid of failure can be a colossal success, lest it be a tiny, intangible undertaking. If it yields an outcome, it is not a failure. In my opinion, failure is the absence of an outcome.

"Do not allow yourself to be disheartened by any failure as long as you have done your best." —Mother Teresa

"He is a failure, he who has never failed, because he has not attempted anything new." —Abdul Shakur

Know this; a mistake is an error that was inappropriately handled. Failure is a mistake that was continuously mishandled. It takes adversity to create success.

Herbert V. Brock puts it best: *"The fellow who never makes a mistake takes his orders from one who does."*

The greater the feat you desire to achieve, the more mental preparation is needed to conquer challenges and endure over time. Making mistakes in life is not only more honorable, but also more useful and adventurous.

Eloise Ristad emphasizes that *"when we give ourselves permission to fail, we at the same time give ourselves permission to excel."*

Lessons From Failure

- I'm only a failure if I make the same mistake twice. It implies that I never learn from my previous mistake.

- Worrying about what other people think of me implies that I have more confidence in their opinion than mine.

- I've come to understand that failure is a necessary step toward success.

- I have learned to carry my past mistakes as a lesson rather than as a burden.
- I have learned to see failure as an event rather than an identity.

- I learned to transform failure into a list of lessons.

- In order to deal with failure more constructively, I learned that I needed to first change my definition of failure.

I have come to realize that, in the end, even if I don't succeed in getting the desired outcome, I would have succeeded in passing the concept on to others who will one day do it differently and eventually succeed.

Physician William Mayo prayed, *"Lord, deliver me from the man who never makes a mistake, and also from the man who makes the same mistake twice."*

PRIORITY

Life doesn't reward effort; it only recognises effort that is directed in the right direction. To advance in life, one must be willing to give up some short-term pleasures now for a secure future. You can't have your cake and eat it too. When you choose to do one thing, you automatically choose to ignore other things. You must give up something in order to obtain something.

Activities don't necessarily equal accomplishment. It's not enough to be busy. In fact, being busy is another form of laziness. You can be busy watching comedy clips, busy watching a football match, busy debating over politicians and politics, busy sleeping... and so forth.

While none of these activities is wrong, the question you should be asking yourself is, "Will this thing I'm doing right now get me closer to my goal?"

Growing up, I knew of a location where a large tree formerly stood. A spot where the majority of adults, including my father, spend their free time. People working in various ministries, government agencies, and non-governmental organizations made up the majority of those seated beneath its shade. People with advanced degrees, master's degrees, and other credentials...

It will amaze you to know that this tree was planted by one of those people sitting under its shade, whose business was just an arm's length away from the shade. While he gist with his friends, he also serves his customers at any slight opportunity.

Guess what? The majority of those people—including my father—are now retired and in the December of their lives, so they no longer congregate around that tree. Why? Because the businessman has scaled up and moved into a larger company venture that now attracts millions in revenue,

You will also be shocked to learn that the businessman in question never had any kind of certification but was able to stay steadfastly focused on his priorities and establish a company that now generates millions in revenue annually.

This got my attention.

This was intriguing to me. How could someone who never received a formal education, came from nothing, and began with almost nothing, not only conquer himself (self-control & self-discipline), but also his surroundings (creating an inviting environment for others to enter & stay), making his business simpler, more enjoyable, and less stressful?

I occasionally consult him for advice on

business and life in general, and if there's one thing I've learned from him, it's to never lose sight of what's most important.

You know, like many others, he could have chosen to close early and join his friends somewhere else, but instead he decided to attract them to himself, and that enabled him to stay longer—making more sales and gaining more profit.

I met him in his new apartment one bright morning and inquired out of curiosity. I'm driven by a strong desire to contribute to improving my life and the world. What advice do you have for me?

Abdul, He began.

It is a fact that all fingers are not equal, but since no one was born with a mark that reads, "He's a thumb, an index, a middle, or little finger..." That implies we have all been given the dignity of choice-to choose which among the fingers we belong.

What you do with your life today determines where you will end up tomorrow. He continued... Although I never got the chance to complete a formal education or earn a degree, I made it a top priority to produce graduates. I never let the fact that I didn't have a formal education stand in my way of going for and attaining my dream.

In his final moments, my father called me. Though I'm not the oldest son, he said to me, "I'm going to leave you with a burden, but I pray that God gives you more wisdom-strength and ability to carry it." He concluded by telling me, Abdul, your father has done his part by sending you to school to acquire a formal education, so it's your turn to show him you appreciate his sacrifices by doing your best to not be a failure.

What exactly do I mean by failing? He queried. You are a failure if your goal is to inherit your father's wealth, possess his house, or drive his car after he passes away. He continued, "My first son has just been sworn in as a medical doctor." Now I want to say to you that, in my opinion, if his greatest accomplishment in life is to buy a home as big as this one (swinging his arm around him), he is a failure. During his lifetime, my father was a wealthy farmer. Nonetheless, he never possessed even one-third of what I have today.

And remember this: Never ever bite the hands that fed you when you were hungry.

It is up to you.

BE ACCOUNTABLE BE RESPONSIBLE

There's an adage that reads, *"God asks no man whether he will accept life." That is not a choice. You must take it. The only question is how. "*

Set the pace by which other people will be measured by it. Self-improvement is not something you do when you feel like it or when you have enough time. It's a daily thing.

Someone said, *"It is easy to dodge our responsibilities, but we cannot dodge the consequences of our responsibilities."*

People rationalise everything, making excuses and blaming everyone but themselves. Anytime things go wrong, instead of looking over our shoulders to point fingers at others or situations to blame, we should instead point at our ego-ask ourselves, "In what way or manner could I have been the cause?" "How could I possibly have drawn this to myself?" "How do I prevent further re-occurrences?"

It's ok to take pride in all of your accomplishments. As long as you're also ready to accept responsibility for anything you do wrong.

There's an African proverb that goes, *"No one goes to the oracle to find out why he's successful."* But if we never blame anyone for our success, how come we blame others for our failure?

Destiny is a choice, not something that happens by accident. It is something that needs to be done; it is not something to be waited for. Some people have an internal locus of control, meaning that they primarily depend on themselves for both their successes and failures in life. Excuses are like dead ends on the road to achievement that we travel. You cannot make the transition from failure to success.

Teachability is demonstrated when you acknowledge your mistakes, look for a clue (no matter how hard it may be), where you've gone wrong, and diligently make an adjustment. And it results in the capacity to alter, develop, and advance in life.

"What you are is not up to you, but who you become is totally your choice."—Abdul Shakur

Although I may not like where I am at the moment, I am accountable for who I am and where I am. My current situation is a direct outcome of my prior decisions and actions, and my future will be a direct result of my prevailing attitudes and actions.

GO FOR CHARACTER OVER REPUTATION

Someone said, *"You don't know what your weaknesses are until you're faced with temptation."*

I had a mid-semester break in my third year of college, and because it was so brief (usually just 10 days), I made the decision to leverage it to catch up on all of my course material, study for tests, and prepare for exams. Because I was a slow learner, I was far behind. It was the 5th week and I still hadn't gotten my monthly stipend. I was unable to call my parents since I was aware that they never missed the due date, and because they hadn't sent anything, that meant they had no money, and calling them might have put them in further debt.

I knew too well that I never had any assistance from anyone other than my two parents (Long life to you, Mum and Dad), so I sat on my back for almost 15 minutes not knowing what to do.

To say it was frustrating would be an understatement. Finally, I summoned courage. I picked up my books and headed for class. I got to the faculty, but most of the classes were locked. After a little scouting, I finally found a class where MSC students were studying, and I entered. I was so hungry that anyone sitting two feet away from me could hear the rumbling and churning of my stomach. I said a silent prayer, "God, if you are there and you are aware of my condition, please help me." A few minutes into my studies, I fell asleep.

My alarm went off just before 1 o'clock, and it was almost time for prayer. After turning off the alarm, I got up to go to the mosque. Suddenly, a girl seated just adjacent to where I was seated pointed to the ground, saying, "Your money is on the floor."

I looked to the ground and found folded currency lying just next to my leg. I swiftly reached out, silently put it into my pocket without looking to see how much it was, and then I and a few other Muslims left right away. On arriving at the mosque entrance after I had performed my ablution, I encountered a beggar who was also blind standing. I reached for the money and found out it was N750 with N500 wrapped around the other two currencies, N200 and N50. I took out the N200 and put it on his plate, then proceeded into the mosque.

Note that everything transpired in a matter of 5 to 6 seconds. When the prayer was finished, I returned to the class to get my things and then returned to the hostel so I could get something to quench my hunger. The guy whose money it was walked in and came straight to me and said, "In a furious tone." "Mr. Man, let me have my money." Then I composed myself and asked, "What money?" Then the girl who pointed the money at me cut in, "The money I pointed to you before you went out." But that was my money, I responded.

He burst out and said, "Don't you joke with me." Bring out that money before I take it out myself.

Fortunately enough, two of the guys with whom we went to the mosque together (and who doubled as his friends) interfered and said, "How much is the money?" The guy replied with N750. Then they faced me and asked, "How much of your own money is there?" Instantly, I recalled I had given out N200, and then I responded. N550 is all I have on me.

They asked me to bring out everything I had on me, which I did, and the only money everyone saw was the N550. The two guys concluded that the money couldn't be his and their main reason was the fact that we went to the mosque together and came back together without losing sight of me.

But was that accurate? NO. I had finished my ablution before they did, but because I headed straight into the mosque, they assumed since I didn't even notice they were watching after me, I couldn't do anything.

After everyone was convinced I wasn't guilty, one of the people who had to watch the entire incident came to me and said, "My friend, I won't advise you to continue sitting here after what has happened." You can't concentrate, and if you let me, I will take you to another class that is much quieter and conducive to learning. “I thanked him and informed him that I would instead return to the hostel.

Since then, no matter how tight my budget was, I've always found a way to donate to charity. Now, don't confuse my generosity for love. Although it has an element to it, the main reason is that I always believe there's a misfortune or trouble coming my way that this charity will surely shield me against.

Even though this incident happened more than 4 years ago, it still brings to mind that character deficiency on my part, and I will carry this guilt with me forever. I have told various Islamic preachers about this incident, and they have all advised me to donate the money to a charity so that the deceased can receive their reward.

A DIFFERENT SCENARIO FROM NAPOLEON HILL'S GOLDEN RULES WILL DRIVE HOME THE LESSONS I'M TRYING TO SHARE

A few months before I began these lessons on applied psychology, I had an experience that gained considerable attention among the interested parties here in the city of Chicago. As I was getting off an elevator in the retail department of A.C. McClure & Company (Chicago's largest book and stationery house), the elevator man allowed the elevator door to slip and catch me between the door and the wall of the elevator.

Besides causing me great pain, the accident tore the sleeve of my coat, damaging it to what looked like beyond repair. I reported the accident to the store manager, Mr. Ryan, who very courteously informed me that I would be reimbursed for the damage done. After a time, the insurance company sent out its agent, looked my coat over, and paid me $40 for the damage.

After the settlement was made and all parties

concerned were satisfied, I took the coat to my tailor, and he made such a neat repair that one could not tell where the coat was torn. The tailor's bill was $2. I had $38 that did not belong to me, yet the insurance company was satisfied, mainly, I suppose, because it got off by paying for less than half the cost of a new suit. A.C. McClure & Company was satisfied because my damage had been made good by their insurance company, and the affair had cost them nothing.

But I was not satisfied! There were many purposes for which I could use that $38. I belonged to it. I had it. There was no one to ever question my right to it or how I acquired it.

Had the insurance company known that the suit could have been so neatly repaired, it probably would have demurred against paying such a large bill, but the question of how the repair would turn out could not be determined in advance.

I argued with my conscience for that $38, but it would not permit me to keep it, so I finally compromised by handing back half of the amount and keeping the other half, on the theory that I had lost considerable time in bringing about the adjustment, and also on the theory that the repair might show up the defective part of the garment later on.

I had to stretch matters considerably in my favour before I felt justified in keeping more than the actual cost of the repairs. When I handed back the money, the representative of McClurg& Company suggested that I just keep the money and forget it, to which I replied, "That's just the trouble; I would like to keep it, but I couldn't forget it!" There was a sound reason why I handed back that $20. That reason had nothing to do with ethics or honesty.

It had nothing to do with the rights of A.C. McClurg& Company or of the insurance company that was protecting McClurg& Company. In arriving at my decision to hand back the money, I never took into consideration either McClurg or the insurance company. They were entirely out of the transaction because they were satisfied. What I took into consideration was my character, knowing as I did that every transaction was influencing my moral fibre, and that character is nothing more or less than the sum of one's habits and ethical conduct.

I knew that I could no more afford to keep that $20 without first having earned the right to it than an apple merchant could afford to place a rotten apple in a barrel of sound ones before storing the barrel away for the winter. I gave back the $20 because I wanted to convince myself that no material could find its way into my character, with my knowledge, except that which I knew to be sound.

I gave back the money because it offered a splendid opportunity for me to test myself and ascertain whether or not I possessed that brand of honesty which prompts a man to be honest for the sake of expedience, or that deeper, nobler, and more worthy brand of honesty which prompts a man to be honest that he may grow stronger and abler to render his fellow men the service that grows out of a desire to be all that he tells the other man to be.

I am convinced that if a man's plans are based upon sound economic principles; if they are fair and just to all whom they affect; and if the man, himself, can throw behind those plans the dynamic force of character and belief in self that grows out of the transactions which have always satisfied his conscience, he will ride on to success, with and by the aid of a tremendous current of force which no power on earth can stop, nay, a force which but few can correctly interpret or understand. - *Napoleon Hill's Golden Rules*

Character can be built to order in the same way that a house can be built to correspond to a set of pre-drawn plans. Your reputation of over thirty years could be ruin in a matter of minutes but your character will keep you immune against compromise and will always keep you afloat when others a long drown.

A BILLION-DOLLAR QUESTION

WHO AM I BECOMING?

Have you ever summoned the courage to look yourself in the eyes and ask yourself, not "Who am I?" but "Who am I becoming?"

It has been said, *"The great thing in this world is not so much where we are at the moment but in what direction we are moving."*

I strongly advise you to do the exercise if you haven't already. Then, step back, give yourself some time to hear what your heart has to say about you, write it down on paper, and assess. If you keep at it long enough, the responses you receive will reveal how far you have deviated from your ideal.

Having done that, now I have a question for you.

In all sincerity,

Is that the person you want to be? Or do you wish you were someone else?

Will you enjoy living in a society where everyone is similar to you? I mean people who think, talk, act and work like you? What kind of homes will we have, and what kind of parents will populate the world?

Will you allow someone who is similar to you to marry your daughter or sister? Or will you trust someone who is similar to you with your wealth, your spouse, or your secrets?

Will the world celebrate or mourn the loss of people like you? Or will the world be a happier and better place to live in because people like you are in leadership positions?

Will the world be proud to have duplicates of your personality and character in its billions of children and youth?

If your answer is in the affirmative, then congratulations! You're on the right track. If not, there's room for improvement.

If you don't like who you are or what you are becoming, you can begin today in the quest for self-improvement. Remember, the largest room in the world is the room for improvement.

You don't need the four walls of a classroom to improve your attitude, your values, your character, your conduct, and your habits.

I'm yet to come across any university or higher institution that operates a faculty of success.

There isn't. Because success begins in the mind.

You can start today by consciously taking a decisive step to change your thinking. Why? Because you are qualified to think. Everyone may not qualify to fight but everyone is qualified to think.

Change what you input into your life and the output will take care of itself.

Be the change you wish to see in the world.

RECOMMENDATION

When I first set out for personal development, I started searching for self-help books. I finally stumbled on the following books and have picked out the once that had the most impact on me to recommend here.

Books on Self-Help:

- Awaken the Giant Within by Anthony Robbins
- The Magic of Thinking Big by David Schwartz
- The Power of Your Subconscious Mind by Joseph Murphy
- As a Man Thinketh by James Allen
- The Power of Positive Thinking by Norman Vincent Peale
- "7 Habits of Highly Effective People" by Stephen R. Covey
- There is a place called Tomorrow by Habu Dawaki

Books on Leadership:

- The Power of Character in Leadership by Myles Munroe
- The 21 irrefutable laws of leadership by John C. Maxwell
- Dale Carnegie's How to Win Friends and Influence People

Books on Finance:

- Rich Dad, Poor Dad
- Think and Grow Rich
- The richest man in Babylon
- The Business of the 21st Century by Robert Kiyosaki
- The School of Money by Olumide Emmanuel
- How to Sell to Nigerians by Akin Alabi

www.ingramcontent.com/pod-product-compliance
Lightning Source LLC
LaVergne TN
LVHW010553160826
845677LV00013B/3115

* 9 7 9 8 8 4 7 7 2 5 8 5 9 *